# ANGELA YARBER

# Queering the American Dream

-A MEMOIR-

ONE QUEER FAMILY WHO LEFT IT ALL
AND THE REVOLUTIONARY WOMEN WHO TAUGHT THEM HOW

**ISBN: 978-1-955581-28-8**

**Book Sales**
100% of sales from this book go to charity. All author royalties fund the Tehom Center, a non-profit teaching about revolutionary women through art, writing, retreats, and academic courses. And Parson's Porch Publishing donates all profits to fulfil its motto of "books to bread" by feeding hungry families. Your purchase helps keeps this work alive. Thank you.

# Other Books by Angela Yarber

*Microaggressions in Ministry: Confronting the Hidden Violence of Everyday Church*
(with Cody Sanders)

*Holy Women Icons Contemplative Coloring Book*

*Dance in Scripture: How Biblical Dancers Can Revolutionize Worship Today*

*Holy Women Icons*

*Tearing Open the Heavens*

*The Gendered Pulpit: Sex, Body, and Desire in Preaching and Worship*

*Embodying the Feminine in the Dances of the World's Religions*

## Dedication

In memory of my little brother, Robert Carl Yarber
November 23, 1983-March 6, 2017

# Prelude

*Ashes to ashes. Dust to dust.*

The chalky remains of a life cut short filled my hands as I watched my faith slip through the cracks between my fingers. As ordained clergy, I've officiated a lot of funerals. For fourteen years, I shaped burnt ash across congregants' foreheads each year before Lent and reminded them that we all come from dust. To dust we shall return. This day, as I officiated my little brother's funeral, I held the ashes of his body in my bare hands. I'd never done this with anyone else's remains, but I wanted to somehow touch him one last time, to feel his pain and let his torment fall through my fingers, as fragments of his bones clung to my palms. Duster to dust. Computer duster killed my brother.

The winds of early March whipped through my grandfather's muscadine vineyard, the place where my brother and I played hide-and-seek throughout our childhood, the sugary scent of late Georgia summer tickling our noses as we ran and swatted mosquitoes. The farm had been a place of solace for both of us and remained so into adulthood, as a tattered family riddled with divorce, addiction, and abuse cobbled together picnic tables long enough to fit all the extended relatives at Thanksgiving and Christmas. Now, we memorialized my thirty-three-year-old brother, as my ninety-year-old grandfather sat small in a folding chair with the scarves, blankets, and coats of all five of his children heaped upon his tiny frame. If it weren't for the death and sadness, the sight of our frail patriarch peeking out from under mounds of outerwear would have been quite comical.

I stood before the folding chairs of family with swipes of my brother's remains smudged across my black dress, as though I had been teaching a thorough lesson at the blackboard of my university classroom and mistakenly leaned against the chalk. A colander was perched atop my head. This was, indeed, comical. And intentional.

You see, my little brother, Carl, was not religious. In fact, he was anti-religious. He embodied his disdain for organized religion with a profound love for the Church of the Flying Spaghetti Monster. As I am a professor of religion, Carl could hold his own with me when discussing world religions,

7

and I would dare say he knew more about Christian history, scripture, and theology than most people who profess the faith. This was in large part because my brother was an intelligent critical thinker, and in small part because he deplored the way most churches treated his queer big sister. But organized religions were not for Carl, so he opted to study and parody them with the Church of the Flying Spaghetti Monster. Started as a protest against right-wing discrimination, the Church of the Flying Spaghetti Monster holds a light-hearted view of religion and jokingly calls its adherents "*pasta*farians." So, the colander is a highly esteemed satirical symbol. You know. Because it drains pasta. In addition to omitting any references to god throughout his funeral, I also opted to wear the colander on my head, passing it around whenever anyone wanted to share a memory or a word of comfort. This probably seems blasphemous to many. As an ordained clergywoman, I think it's pretty damn funny.

I needed the levity. Other clergy colleagues offered to officiate, knowing how emotional I would be and seeking to provide me with the care I was extending to so many others. But I couldn't trust anyone with the words and gestures, rituals and lamentations for honoring my little brother.

Trembling under March clouds, the vineyard behind me, farmhouse beside me, family before me, and shiny metal colander rattling above me, I couldn't help but wonder, "How in the hell did we get here? And how can we survive this?"

**How'd We Get Here?**

In many ways, that's what this book is about. How in the hell did we get here? It should just be a travel memoir, not a eulogy. For eighteen months, my wife, toddler, and I roamed the country as my brother's addiction morphed into a bigger and bigger beast. In this meandering travelation-turned-funeral narrative, the lives, legends, and legacies of the revolutionary holy women I paint and write about were—and continue to be—my guides. They are how I survived this, and I believe they can help you survive and thrive, too. No matter your grief or loss.

It was the myth of Lilith leaving the garden of Eden that gave me the courage to leave a job that was assaulting my soul. It was the passionate nomad Freya Stark's sentiment that, "it's the beckoning that counts, not the clicking latch behind you" that called me out of ordinary life to wonder and wander as a form of vocational discernment. It was Pauli Murray's intrepid resilience as she faced overt discrimination because of her race, gender, sexuality, and gender identity that buoys my work as an artist, author, and Executive Director of a fledgling non-profit that is trying to make substantive changes for marginalized women and our access to empowerment, inspiration, and beauty.

More than quotable phrases or clichés, however, is the way these revolutionary women form a subversive sisterhood of saints that surrounds and upholds all queer women seeking to live and work outside the box of white supremacist cisheteropatriarchy, outside the bounds of the American dream. Because of them, not only can we work outside this dream, but we can begin to dismantle it. How in the hell did we get here? With a lot of dismantling.

And that's a hefty weight to haul through the world with a colander on your head. Leaving. Roaming. Dismantling. Grieving. Creating. With a toddler in tow. Throughout this wandering, I share with you not only the stories of my traveling family in all our queer, broken, addicted, faithless glory. I also share with you the guides, the revolutionary women whose footsteps paved the way, offering inspiration and empowerment to anyone bold enough to follow. Sixteen women, to be exact. One historical woman and one mythological woman for each phase of the journey: Leaving, Vermont, the Southeast, Crossing the Country East to West along the southern border, Hawai'i, Crossing the Country West to East along the northern border, the North Carolina mountains, and back to Hawai'i again.

Lilith and Jarena Lee, Sophia and Freya Stark, Mary and Pauli Murray, Our Lady of Guadalupe and Gloria Anzaldúa, Pelé and Dorothy Day, Guanyin and Audre Lorde, Sarasvati and Sojourner Truth, Frida Kahlo and the Goddess of Grief offered lessons in courage, integrity, hope, creativity, rage, care, interconnectedness, and resilience along the way. In fact, they paved the way. Because of them, I could. And do. And am. In the most beautiful or gut-wrenching places, they emboldened my queer little family. I painted them and wrote about them. And I now I share some of their stories, and mine, with you.

Each of these revolutionary women embodied a particular virtue that emboldened my travels, giving me strength and comfort in the wake of my brother's death. I believe they can do the same for you. If the American dream isn't working for you, if you've been excluded, ignored, or erased from the dream touted by so many, these are the stories you need to hear. If you want to invoke the radical imagination necessary to create a better world, I encourage you to keep reading. Courage, integrity, hope, creativity, rage, care, interconnectedness, and resilience are waiting for you. These revolutionary women, and my queer family's wanderings, taught me how to embody these virtues in order to have the radical imagination to queer the American dream. Now, I share these lessons with you, so that, together, we can create a better world.

**The Green Plastic Bin.**

You see, I began painting these intrepid guides in 2008, giving traditional iconography a folk-feminist twist by painting revolutionary women otherwise overlooked in spiritual traditions, history, and mythology. But their role in my life goes back much farther.

In 1999, I was hunkered in a Russian Orthodox Church as the American Embassy was bombed, gazing at the brooding, whitewashed faces of male saints glaring back at me. I kept asking myself, Where are all the women? In 2005, as I rode a camel up Mt. Sinai to experience the sensory overload of Saint Catherine's Monastery—which housed the oldest collection of Christian icons in the world—I could find only two women crammed among them. Where were all the women? With my eyes fixed upon thousands of golden statues at the Temple of Thousand Buddhas in Thailand a few years later, not one woman could be found. And I continued to ask, Where are all the women?

This question—Where are all the women—continues to guide much of my painting and writing, as I canonize marginalized women into the subversive sisterhood of saints. In the paintings, their hearts occupy the bulk of the canvas, and I accompany every painting with the cry of each woman's heart scrawled poetically across the canvas. When we left for our travels, I had sold most of my nearly 100 icons. The remaining few, fifteen to be exact, were waiting to be hung in an exhibit. I couldn't bear to leave them in storage. So, I carefully placed all the icons in an enormous green plastic bin that would occupy far too much space in our camper during our travels. In all our wanderings, the hearts of these folk-feminist icons remained, beating truth and courage, audacity and compassion from the green plastic bin wedged in our storage compartment.

Because these women did revolutionary things that upset the status quo during their times on earth, they stir similar impulses in me. Alongside their stories, and mine, you will find the ways in which their virtues evoke social justice today. Whether it's a contemporary issue, such as environmental racism, or a timely event, such as the Pulse Massacre, I do not hold back my rage or longing. Nor did they. Accordingly, each chapter contains three intersecting stories: 1. my queer family's travelations, 2. a historical woman's life who paved the way, and 3. a mythological woman's legacy who paved the way. All this is simply too much for a green plastic bin to hold, so it spilled out over these pages and filled this book.

Historian Gerda Lerner claimed, "Women's history is the primary tool for women's emancipation." One cannot tell the stories of these women without also telling the stories of liberation they incite today. More than mere soapboxes or miles traveled, these are the cries of their hearts, and mine. My words may wander from time to time, but within all the wandering stories is the collective heartbeat of revolutionary women, longing for emancipation. Invite this longing to guide you.

It is the stories of these subversive sister saints that kept me going. Whether it was traversing jaw dropping landscapes with my wife and toddler or wailing in despair as my brother's addiction spiraled, these women, and the woman I call my wife, upheld me. And I believe their stories can uphold you, too. Hidden in the crevices of our canons at best, strategically erased at worst, theirs are the revolutionary stories we all deserve to hear. If only we listen, we just may queer the American dream.

**Queer.**

With upspoken stories in mind, it's worth a brief pause to make a little note about language. I will often refer to us as my "queer little family," or discussing "queering" dreams, and I imagine this will have plenty of folks—straight and queer alike—wondering what exactly I mean by this. When I employ this word, I mean three overlapping things. First, I use queer as an umbrella term for the LGBTQIA+ (lesbian, gay, bisexual, transgender, queer, questioning, intersex, asexual, allied, and more) community; this avoids the inevitable "alphabet soup," forgetting or misplacing a letter in the acronym, and it includes both sexuality and gender identity without excluding either. Second, the use of the term queer draws from the academic discipline of queer theory, which seeks to dismantle hierarchical binaries, such as male/female, gay/straight, man/woman by exploring the interstitial space between binaries. Third, the use of queer also reclaims the once derogatory term by harkening back to the dictionary definition of "queer," which is to "intentionally transgress or subvert." Spirituality, sexuality, and gender identity is queer insomuch as it intentionally transgresses oppressive boundaries or limitations used to exclude the LGBTQIA+ community. Of course, all these usages are much more nuanced, but these three understandings give you a general idea of what I mean when referring to myself or my family. Queer is both something you can be and something you can do. To queer something—the American dream, perhaps—is to subvert it, turn it on its head, question and dismantle it.

Feminist writer Adrienne Rich claims, "Whatever is unnamed, undepicted in images…whatever is misnamed as something else, made difficult-to-come-by, whatever is buried in the memory by the collapse of meaning under an inadequate or lying language—this will become, not only unspoken, but unspeakable." Unnamed disenfranchised grief, undepicted images of revolutionary women from history and myth, stories buried by the lying language of patriarchy, and the difficult-to-come-by queer traveling family losing our faith across the American landscape will no longer remain unspoken, for in these words and stories, in this book, these women speak again. I will no longer tolerate inadequate language.

My queer little family muddled our way around the country, experiencing grief, joy, fear, longing, love, and the impacts of addiction. Fifteen revolutionary women icons squeezed into a green plastic bin were our faithful travel companions. Together, we pilgrimaged a country whose landscape caused our jaws to routinely drop in wonder, yet whose policies routinely failed us. And we found that the people of this country are somewhere in between, causing our wandering hearts to oscillate between wonderous beauty and sheer heart break.

**Disclaimer.**

Perhaps you're thinking, "Wow, how'd they do it and where do I sign up?!" Or maybe, "Great, another story about a white woman traveling to find herself. Who is she to teach about these revolutionary women, many of whom are women of color (WOC)?"

12

Perhaps, "Were they trying to commit career suicide?"
Even, "Who the hell raises their toddler in a camper gallivanting all over the country?"

Believe me when I say that we asked all these questions, too. And still do, to some extent. There's no denying the privilege that accompanies this adventure. Is traveling throughout the United States as a queer couple— two women and a toddler—easy and safe? Not exactly, particularly amidst an election cycle that routinely demonized queers and ignored the safety of women. Did we do everything on a tiny budget, living simply, and making a lot of sacrifices? Yes. Did we work really hard to make it happen? Sure. But our white skin and tremendous education also afforded us a lot of privileges unavailable to many others. As we traveled and planned and explored, we remained acutely aware of this, hoping to balance our sincere desire to wonder and wander with our responsibility and calling to make the world a more just and beautiful place for all. It's possible that, if everyone committed to creating a more just and beautiful world for all, people like my little brother wouldn't turn to ash.

And when it comes to sharing the stories of revolutionary women from history and myth, almost all of whom have different cultural backgrounds than I do, here is where I land. The lives, legends, and legacies of these forerunners have been altogether ignored and excluded in most history books, stained glass windows, iconography, and public histories. As a queer feminist and scholar, it is my responsibility to shout their stories from the rooftops. Because their stories affect social change, evoke revolution, and embolden today's women to keep striving and thriving. Simultaneously, I acknowledge that their stories are not my own; as a cis, white, woman, there are elements of their struggles which I can never grasp. It is my hope that glimpses into their narratives will spark you to learn more. Read their books, research their lives, follow in their footsteps. Not just mine. As a queer white feminist, I am called to shine an excavating light on the WOC who have paved the way. May my book allow this light to guide you to follow their revolutionary lead. If you do, together, we just may queer the American dream.

## Introduction:

# Courage
# Lilith and Jarena Lee

*"I've been absolutely terrified every moment of my life—and I've never let it keep me from doing a single thing I wanted to do."—Georgia O'Keeffe*

Everything smells like a rainy backpacking trip. Before our child was born, my wife, Elizabeth, and I did a fair amount of backpacking, and we took Riah camping in the middle of the redwoods before he was even ten months old. It's a smell we're accustomed to, but it's not exactly how I envisioned starting this adventure. With an enormous green canoe strapped precariously to the top of a 2004 Explorer, we've been towing our new home—a pop-up camper named Freya—from North Carolina in the direction of Vermont for three days of solid rain. Intent on communing with one of my patron saints of painting, Georgia O'Keeffe, we've pulled into a rather swank campground in Lake George, the place where O'Keeffe summered and painted for many years. We'll camp here for two nights before heading to our summer gig in Vermont.

A retired woman in a star-spangled blouse meets us at the gate. "Do you mean to tell me that you girls are traveling for a year in a pop-up camper with a toddler? Have you lost your minds? Where are your husbands?!" she asks incredulously, her accent laced with Long Island. With absurd smiles stretched across our road weary faces and rain soaking our hair, we respond with the enthusiasm of new travelers, "That's the plan!" After rattling off the list of things you *can't* do in the fancy campground, she arches her eyebrow skeptically at our rig as we back into our site. It takes three tries.

As the rain pummels the canvas, Elizabeth begins the hour-long process of popping up the camper while Riah and I take off to explore the campground. He splashes wildly through puddles, sometimes babbling one of his eight words, while I take note of our neighbors and their expensive RVs, complete with wooden porches, yard décor, hanging baskets overflowing with summer flowers, and a lot of American flags. Not really our scene, but we're excited that—after a year of planning—the adventure is officially beginning.

So, we unhitch the camper, and as I pull the Explorer out of the way, the check engine light comes on. This is not the best way to begin a year on the road, especially since we just had the car fully serviced one week prior. I call and make an appointment at a local shop for the next morning. "We'll have to unstrap the canoe in order to take the car to the shop," I inform Elizabeth.

"That fucking canoe." This would become Elizabeth's refrain for at least the next three months. Apparently, she doesn't enjoy paddling quite as much as I do. We put the check engine light out of our minds and turn to something more urgent: sleep.

This is technically our first night in the camper, and we haven't quite figured out where our 20-month-old child is going to sleep. We'll sleep in a king size bed on one end of the 140 sq/ft pop-up. There is a Queen size bed on the other end that we've already dubbed Riah's "romp around" space. It seems logical for him to snooze there, but we are worried that, since he'd always slept in a crib, he might tumble out in the night. After ridiculous attempts at perching the pack-and-play on top of the mattress, we decide to barricade the sides of the bed with luggage to prevent a midnight fall.

We settle Riah into his romp-around room, and he sleeps fitfully. We cozy up in our damp bed and listen to the rain batter the canvas of the camper. It's stinky and soggy, and mud coats much of the camper floor. There is a thirteen-foot green canoe that needs to be taken off the Explorer by 8am, and I'll have to run the five miles back from the mechanic's because they don't offer a shuttle service. And yet those ridiculous grins remain plastered across our faces as we doze off in our dank little camper, dreaming of the adventure that awaits us.

If someone had described this scene at Lake George—pouring rain, wet pop-up camper, fussy toddler, broken car, heavy canoe, an abundance of American flags—I don't think I would have traded our comfortable bed in the historic craftsman nestled within perfect walking distance of downtown that we called home for three years. But I did. And I would again. No questions about it.

15

It didn't begin with Lake George. Actually, it's difficult to determine what exactly prompted the seemingly wild decision to quit our jobs, sell our home, and travel for eighteen months with our toddler in a camper. Throughout our nearly decade-long relationship, Elizabeth and I had always talked about "living differently." Whatever the hell that means. These initial conversations took place in Berkeley while we were working on our Ph.D.s. With the world at our fingertips, time on our hands, privilege seeping through our highly educated pores, and little in our bank accounts, I dreamed of a life untethered. But academia and a call to ministry tied me down. Bidding our beloved Bay goodbye, we moved to North Carolina for work with our newly minted doctorates. I was a pastor. Elizabeth, a professor. That lasted fewer than three years.

It wasn't the plan. And I'm big on plans. I write them down, color-coded, with carefully articulated goals affixed neatly to each stage of the plan, a strict timeline enforced for achievement. I'm a rare author who has never asked for an extension on a deadline. Because that's not part of the plan.

We made North Carolina home. Bought a house. Started an adoption process. I thought I'd serve that church for ten years. But it became toxic. Church often has that effect on women and queers. And I'm both of those things. The file folder of hate mail grew thicker and the sexist and heterosexist microaggressions raged within my own congregation. It was ultimately the microaggressions that did me in. Spiritually spent, I went on a retreat for artists and activists, and began to heal. In healing, I discerned the time had come for me to follow Lilith's footsteps, climbing the "garden's walls" to find liberation and work outside the confines of church and academy.

## Climbing the Garden's Walls

Lilith has been a misunderstood, appropriated, and redeemed woman throughout the ages. Many feminists claim her as an empowering figure in Jewish mythology, her story reclaimed by contemporary artists such as Sarah McLachlan, who created the all-women music tour, "Lilith Fair," which I attended multiple times as a teenager. Others have alleged that Lilith was a demon who seduced men and strangled children in the night. Quite the contrast, eh?

According to the Midrash of Jewish feminist Judith Plaskow, God created Adam and Lilith from the same earth. Tired of Adam demanding that she

be subservient to him, Lilith left the Garden of Eden. She was later befriended by Eve and her legacy of empowering women continues today.
In the Jewish tradition, midrash is akin to climbing inside the story—inside the Torah—and imagining what happened in the places where the text offers no description; it is the space between the letters, the creative imagination within the narrative that makes the story come alive.

Plaskow's powerful Midrash stems from a myth that has shifted over time. There is no single Lilith story, but many different stories must be sifted and sorted to determine who Lilith truly is and was. She appears explicitly only once in the Hebrew Bible (Isaiah 34:14) in a list of wild animals in desolate land. She is not described but named simply: "Lilith." Some scholars surmise that the Lilith myth was so well-known by Isaiah's audience that there was no need to offer any explanatory words.

In Talmudic literature, Lilith is associated with the creation story in a manner similar to Plaskow's Midrash. Here she is also banished from the Garden. In the *Alphabet of Ben Sira* (7th-11th centuries) Lilith is presented as Adam's first wife. When she refuses to lie with Adam during sex, she calls out the name of god and flies away to an evil place filled with demons. By the end of the Talmudic period, the demonic and seductive elements of the Lilith myth were solidified. So, in the writings of the Kabbalah, Lilith is primarily understood to be a seductress and child-killer. Regarding this reputation, some feminist scholars assert that the vilification of Lilith intensifies over time because Lilith is perceived to be more and more powerful. The more powerful Lilith is perceived to be, the more evil her portrayal. What Plaskow's Midrash creates, redeems, and affirms is that Lilith left what was hurting and oppressing her and lived into who she was called to be: one who empowered women.

Interpreting Plaskow's feminist midrash with a queer lens offers further redemptive potential, particularly if we remember the many times we queer folk have been pushed outside the "garden's walls" because we are not welcome, we do not belong, or we cannot follow the rules of heteronormativity. In fact, some queer biblical scholars claim that Lilith came back to garden's walls, not simply to befriend and attempt to liberate Eve, but for the two women to fall in love. How many times, in history, myth, and everyday life, have queer women been pushed out of the garden, while others claimed that they chose to willingly go? How much of a choice does one have when the garden's vines are strangling you? They choked out Lilith, and they choked out me.

Like many clergywomen, I faithfully served the church for nearly fourteen years. After eleven years of ministry, I accepted a call to become Pastor for Preaching and Worship at a Baptist church on the campus of a research university. Upon hiring me, we became the only Baptist church in the country with two out lesbians as head pastors. My pulpit was free. My calling to justice, inclusion, and radical hospitality affirmed. I loved—and continue to love—the staff and the people who call this church home. I loved—and continue to love—preaching. But sexism and heterosexism have their way of creeping into the most unlikely of places. And the inner-workings of power and privilege make dealing with these "isms" ever more difficult.

Though the church wouldn't tolerate overt and blatant sexism or homophobia from within the congregation—and spoke out against the overt forms I received in hate mail—microaggressive sexisms and heterosexisms continued to exist, flourishing in spaces we thought were safe, affirming, and progressive. Microaggressions are everyday slights, insults, or invalidations directed at marginalized groups—persons of color, sexual minorities, women, etc—by individuals who typically have good intentions and are decent, moral, thoughtful persons who may not be fully aware of their privileged positions of power. Psychologists who focus on cultural diversity issues claim that microaggressions build up over time, causing stress, pain, and anxiety for marginalized persons.

After months and months of trying to address these issues, my health continued to decline. I reread Barbara Brown Taylor's *Leaving Church* and I thought a lot about Lilith. How did she garner the courage to leave the "safety" of the Garden for the great unknown? I began to paint.

The colors of Eden filled my canvas, as a strong woman walked left, reaching out toward the unknown that lies beyond the Garden, the place she has called home. Lilith's heart cries out to us,

> *With Eden behind her,*
> *She stood her ground,*
> *Her heart beating*
> *Freedom and dignity*
> *For all women.*

Not knowing what existed beyond the place I called "home" for nearly fourteen years, I resigned from my position in a coveted, progressive Baptist pulpit. Since I offered my resignation, many have asked me if I think the church—any church—can exist with*out* sexism and heterosexism. Called, ordained, degreed, and with over a decade dedicated to working to overcome it, I'm afraid my answer is a faint, but hopeful, "I don't know." The Garden—the church—can be a beautiful place. Lurking behind those beautiful flowers, it can also be a place with tangled vines that strangle the least among us. Like Lilith, I had to climb over the Garden's walls and find out what's on the other side. In order to save my soul, I had to leave the church. In order to save her soul, I believe Lilith had to leave the Garden.

As the stacks of hate mail grew higher, I resigned and taught at the university part-time, relying on my writing and artwork to supplement our once combined six-figure income. I loved teaching. Elizabeth liked it alright. I published some books and had some art shows. We got involved in community organizing. Our life was nice. We matched for an open adoption and welcomed our newborn into a comfortable, safe, creative home in a relatively diverse neighborhood. Life was fine. Good, even. Yet the beckoning continued. Lilith helped me climb the garden's walls. Now, I had to trust her to lead me into the unknown.

**The Beckoning.**

Though traditional academia and local church ministry contributed much to who we are, we realized that they confined our wider vision for our family and our world. We'd always wanted to open a small non-profit retreat center but thought this couldn't be our reality until we paid our dues to the academy and church; it was a retirement dream, we believed. When I resigned from my toxic job as pastor, we began to reevaluate the life we were living. Did we really need a 1,900 square foot house and two vehicles? Did we truly want to work just so we could pay the bills necessary to live this way? When Riah was born, one would think that we'd have really settled in, hunkered down with the baby and mortgage and routine.

But I convinced Elizabeth to take a month-long road trip when Riah was nine months old. We started at a friend's wedding in Denver and then hiked our way through Utah, visited friends in California, pitched our tent inside a redwood tree, picked blackberries up the Oregon coast, and ended with another friend's wedding in Washington. Then we flew back to life-as-usual, knowing that things could never be the same. I was offered a prestigious job in D.C. In many ways, it would have been my dream job as a queer activist, but the more I learned and discerned, the more confident we became that accepting this job would entail me raising our child over Skype, always on the road and rarely with family. I turned it down, not knowing what might come next vocationally. And for the first time in my career, I was genuinely ok with that.

Elizabeth was an ethics professor, and she strongly disagreed with the ethics of the university where she taught. I was cobbling together teaching three or four classes per semester between the Women's, Gender, and Sexuality Studies Department and Divinity school, but still wasn't full-time, while also writing, painting, and teaching fitness classes at the gym. We traded off parenting and had little time together as a family. Life was good, relatively comfortable, and even meaningful. But we wanted more. We wanted our values to better coincide with our practices, for our theory to be engaged, for our intersectional ecofeminism to be embodied and lived fully.

Intersectional feminism, a term coined by Kimberlé Crenshaw, refers to feminism that doesn't merely focus on gender equality, but also the intersections of race, class, ability, sexuality, gender identity, religion, and all the other isms often used to exclude and marginalize; justice for all, not just justice for straight, white women. Ecofeminism, put most simply, is the bridge between ecology and feminism, acknowledging that there is a direct relationship between how we treat the earth and how we treat marginalized women. We taught these things in our classrooms. I preached them from the pulpit and wrote about them in esoteric books that other academics sometimes read, but that mostly cushioned my curriculum vitae. We wanted our lives to reflect these values more fully. Not just in recycling, or marching in the women's march, or wearing a Black Lives Matter t-shirt, or talking about war-tax resistance, or posting lots of woke articles on social media, or trying really hard to be vegan and succeeding 90% of the time. But more fully and robustly. And maybe we could have done this in our historic craftsman while I tried to teach body-positive and fat-inclusive yoga to a bunch of skinny white ladies at the gym. Maybe Lilith could have subverted Eden from within. Maybe?

But that's not how this story goes. And it isn't how this adventure began. It began with a wild plan and big leap. We decided to sell our home, leave our jobs, and follow the beckoning…wherever it might lead. For a year, we researched campground hosting positions, caretaking opportunities, Working on Organic Farm programs, Artist in Residencies, volunteer and work-exchange options, along with securing a couple of freelance writing and online teaching gigs, speaking events, and art shows that could sustain the $1,000 monthly income we'd need to survive. By living in different beautiful places, learning new skills, and thoughtfully considering our life goals, we hoped to complete the adventure prepared to open a small retreat center with an organic garden, a non-profit to house my painting and writing. Leading retreats, partnering with universities and seminaries to offer land-based intensive classes, providing hospitality to the marginalized, and living sustainably, creatively, justly: these were the goals. The skills we hoped to develop throughout this adventure would better equip us to achieve our future goals, and practicing these skills along the way would help us discern whether this was the best path forward for our family. At least, that was the new plan.

After the month-long road trip and subsequent D.C. job offer I didn't accept, it was settled. We were doing this. We were going to resign from our jobs, sell our house, buy a little camper, and start some kind of wild adventure. We knew we wanted to travel, likely with the end goal of finding land to open the non-profit of our dreams. We wanted to learn some new skills and explore beautiful places along the way. The question was, where to begin?

My penchant for color-coded charts and lists helped shape the wild dream. Elizabeth began researching volunteer work-exchange opportunities in National Parks and Forests. I reached out to my network of contacts in church, academia, and the arts. These options became one chart. Everything we needed to do to get there became another: selling the house, vehicles, getting rid of a lot of stuff and determining what goes into storage, securing some additional income to prepare us for life on the road, researching and purchasing a camper and vehicle to tow it. Within the chart were more charts and lists, complete with deadlines. An appendix to both charts were dates when all our family and friends wanted to visit before we left, along with appointments in the North Carolina mountains to look at potential land for the retreat center. Because that's where we figured we'd end up.

To sell the house and get a good return, we made a list of all the projects around the house we'd need to do. From September through March, we had a long list of home improvement project deadlines. After years of watching home improvement television, and the generational privilege of having a retired realtor in Elizabeth's family, we felt certain of our abilities to "appeal to buyers." Fortunately, the realtor who sold us our house three years prior had become a friend and offered free advice for when and how to sell. We were tremendously lucky because we bought at the bottom of the market, and our neighborhood was quite desirable. She encouraged us to sell by owner, hoping for a return that would fund our adventure and offer some savings for creating the non-profit.

After replacing old appliances with stainless steel ones from an outlet, haggling prices for floor models with the smallest of scratches, resurfacing butcher block counters, and painting all our 100-year-old cabinets white, we renovated our old kitchen for under $2,000. Then we cleaned and spray-painted vents, repainted the porch, depersonalized the house, and mulched the yard. All-in we spent around $3,000 and a lot of sweat fixing up the house, often with our baby strapped to one of our chests. We listed the house online at 9pm the week our realtor-friend recommended as the best for our area; the listing including an open house for the upcoming weekend, and I planned to place the yard sign in our freshly mulched flower beds the next morning.

At 7:30am the next day I received a call from a realtor.
"Have you sold your house yet?" he asked.
"Uhm, no," I replied quizzically, "we just listed it last night."
"I have a buyer who wants to make an offer higher than list price. She's from New York, but used to live here and wants to move into your neighborhood. She says this is her dream home and she doesn't want to lose it to another buyer. I just need to come by this morning and confirm that your photos match the reality of the home."
I rattled my brain to see if a friend or family member might be playing a practical joke on me. Surely this couldn't be real. I pinched myself to make sure I wasn't dreaming. Could this be one of my brothers?
"Did Carl and Josh put you up to this?" I asked sardonically.
"Excuse me, ma'am," the realtor responded.
"Is this a joke or are you being for real?" I demanded.
"My client is quite serious about her offer. She has been looking for a month and contacted me late last night upon seeing your listing online. She

plans to book a flight soon so she can see the house in person. Are you amenable to my seeing the home today?" he responded, without an ounce of humor.

"Of course. Ok. That sounds great." I muttered in disbelief.

I ran downstairs and wrote on the chalkboard that graced our new stainless-steel refrigerator a quote from a fabulous travel writer who also left everything to follow the beckoning: Frances Mayes. "The world cracks open for those who dare to dream." The realtor came, the offer was made official, we determined a date for closing, and I returned the For Sale sign to the hardware store. The universe (or goddess, or privilege, or happenstance) was confirming our decision. That night when we were in bed, Elizabeth squeezed my hand and looked at me. "We're doing this," she said. This, too, would become our refrain throughout our wild adventure. We're doing this.

## Downsizing.

While preparing the house to be sold, we researched campers and decided that a pop-up would likely be a good fit. Though we'd have really liked to fix up a vintage airstream or buy something used, we didn't have the time or skills to repair anything, especially while working, parenting a toddler, and planning everything related to the adventure, so we settled on buying an affordable model and hoping for the best. This involved our first foray into RV culture, a place where I never imagined residing. We coordinated visiting a few RV shops with Riah's naptime, taking turns walking in and out of campers while salesmen (they were always men) scratched their heads, questioning whether we were friends or sisters. Because it never crossed their minds that we were a family and that Elizabeth and I were married. Given the state of LGBTQ rights and acceptance in North Carolina at the time, we opted not to correct the salesmen in the rural areas that house RV shops.

Dear friends volunteered to babysit so we could enter—with a mixture of trepidation and curiosity—the apex of camper culture: an RV show. Just outside Charlotte, sellers of RVs, campers, fifth wheels, and travel trailers journeyed throughout the Southeast to hawk their wares at retirees and families in search of summer vacation plans. There was absolutely nothing about it that resembled camping. We are a camping and backpacking couple, which usually means that we explore with our tiny tent securely snugged within the backpack on our backs, a can of beans and water bottles weighing down our small frames as we plough through parts of the Appalachian Trail or kiss banana slugs in the Santa Cruz mountains. We are lesbians, after all. This wasn't camping. This was Vegas on wheels.

There was a map that guides potential buyers throughout the lots and warehouses filled with these small, and not-so-small, traveling homes. The section of pop-up campers comprised a tiny corner staffed with only one salesman. I imagine he was not so happy with his post, coveting the fat commissions of his competitors. Before heading that way, we decided to gawk at some of the luxury RVs for fun. Complete with multiple televisions, outdoor movie screens, granite counter tops, leather recliners and sectionals, washer/dryers, and separate bedrooms for four, these behemoths were priced substantially higher than our house and required a commercial license to drive them. There's nothing like getting out into nature with $300 worth of gas in the tank and cable television. But, as Elizabeth reminded me, many people, including us, don't just use these traveling homes for so-called glamping, but as their full-time lodging; if a retiree wants to travel in comfort after a lifetime of work, I can't really blame them. But I still don't think it should be called camping. And the environmental impact is an entirely differently story.

We settled on an affordable pop-up that had a toilet, sink, and small refrigerator. It seemed like it would fit our little family perfectly and wouldn't be as intimating to tow as a big rig. The salesman pointed us to a dealership nearby and we scheduled an appointment to buy. I haggled over the phone and we agreed upon a price.

Also completely perplexed by the two women purchasing a pop-up together, the salesman (yes, yet another man) filled out our paperwork incorrectly multiple times and appeared totally bamboozled that our husbands weren't arriving any moment to hitch up the rig and tow it home. As we merged onto the freeway, Elizabeth repeated the phrase that seemed to become our adventure's motto: we're doing this. I looked into the rearview mirror and our little home chugged along behind us. If I were the New Age spirituality-type, I'd swear Lilith was flying behind us.

With the pop-up nestled next to our historic home, we finished planning the bulk of the year. First, Elizabeth secured us three months as campground hosts in the Green Mountain National Forest of Vermont.

We'd have free power to plug the camper in, but no running water. Next, we'd continue volunteer campground hosting in Southern Virginia while I had an art show and retreats to lead in North Carolina for autumn. A month in Atlanta visiting family would fade into popping up along the southern border from Georgia to California throughout the winter holidays. We'd hang another exhibit and store the camper with former congregants in California so we could fly to Hawai'i for me to be a scholar-in-residence at a farm. And then the plans were loose, with hopes we'd figure out details before then. We'd likely slowly make our way back across the country along the northern route, ending back in North Carolina where we intended to buy land to create the non-profit retreat center we'd been dreaming of. Queering the American dream.

Before all this, we needed to save and earn some money. In the month before leaving, Elizabeth taught two summer courses, I taught one, and I doubled up on teaching fitness and dance classes. After packing, storing, selling, donating, and planning, we were nearly ready. Throughout that busy month, every one of our child's eight grandparents squeezed in a visit, and so did his birth parents. Which brings me to another caveat important for your understanding moving forward. What's a birth parent?

**Adoption.**

We have an open adoption, and though adoption is always a form of trauma, ours is one that likely involves the least amount of trauma possible. Riah's birth parents knew from the outset they never planned to have children. Adoption was their top choice while she finished her MA and he his PhD. Upon realizing that the adoption agencies in her state wouldn't work with same-sex couples, his birth mother was furious, resolutely researching other open agencies. And she found us.

First, we emailed. Then we talked over the phone and Skype. Then we drove ten hours to meet them in Michigan to attend a doctor's visit. This was all as I was leaving my job. We officially "matched," which is akin to getting engaged. Elizabeth and I stayed in Michigan for two weeks before and after Riah's birth, while all four of us worked together with social workers and attorneys. His birth parents remain an incredibly important part of our lives, and they function much like and aunt and uncle. For us, open adoption was yet another way we wanted to queer and subvert what it means to be family. And we couldn't have found two people more amazing,

25

smart, athletic, and kind to welcome into our family. It's not perfect, and not necessarily easy. But queering usually isn't.

Since our house was packed into boxes and we no longer had a spare bed, we all decided it would be fun for Riah's birth parents to have the inaugural stay in the pop-up camper, so we booked them a site at a local campground. Joining them—and soon, us—were those fifteen of my holy women icon paintings, already nestled in their green plastic tub in the storage compartment.

As Riah's birthparents played endless games of peek-a-boo, we hung my icons all over the pop-up, a cavalcade of color exploding off the metal siding and canvas top. Crooked and falling, messy and holy—kind of like us—these icons transformed our little camper into a temple of sorts, a sacred space reminding us to pause, show gratitude, and be bold. As you may imagine, we received our fair share of strange glances. But we also shared some meaningful and unlikely conversations with women now emboldened by these brightly painted saints to do more justice, live more creatively, and be a bit more revolutionary.

As I pinned the final icon to the awning—Jarena Lee—I reflected on the time I spent healing following my toxic pastorate, preparing for full-time travel, and questioning whether I was just leaving church, or leaving faith altogether. Something stirred within as Jarena and I stood face to face, two preachers walking in opposite directions.

**Vocation.**

Jarena Lee spent thirty years as an itinerant preacher and was the first black woman to be licensed to preach through the African Methodist Episcopal (AME) church. Despite the fact that the AME issued a definitive ruling that women were *not* permitted to preach in 1852, Lee spent the bulk of her adult life preaching. Jarena Lee's struggle to preach is a familiar story in nineteenth-century American Protestantism, even though the Second Awakening ushered in a period of intense religious revival; with camp meetings around every corner, there was an unprecedented opportunity for women to preach. Like Jarena Lee, though, they weren't paid, ordained, or protected.

Lee moved from New Jersey to Philadelphia when she was 21 and told the famous Richard Allen that she was called by the Spirit to preach. Since the AME's book of discipline didn't say anything about women preachers yet, Allen asked her to hold off for a bit. So, she did what many frustrated women called to preach did; she married a preacher. Six years into the marriage her husband died, and she knew she could no longer ignore her calling.

So, Jarena Lee left her two children in the care of people at church and hit the road. Her journals indicate that in one year alone she walked 2,325 miles and preached 178 sermons; that's more than three sermons per week and six miles per day. And before we pass judgment on Lee for leaving her children in the care of others, it's important to acknowledge her context. According to homiletics scholar Anna Carter Florence:

> "Preaching is a way of living and speaking in right relationship with God. It is a way of standing in one's own life, before God and others. A preacher who denies this denies her very self; she goes down into the pit. She gets swallowed by the whale. She gets tossed this way and that until she relinquishes false notions of what her life should be and submits to God. And God does not adhere to human articulations of polity: God calls whom God will. If the preacher is a poor black woman in antebellum Philadelphia in the year 1811, a woman whom no one will believe and for whom living out the call will be unimaginably difficult, so be it: God does not call preachers to *be believed*. God calls preachers to *preach*. Lee had tried standing in someone else's life; it hadn't worked. She was ready to stand on her own." (Florence, *Preaching as Testimony*, 44)

So, standing on her own two feet, sanctified and called, Jarena Lee was led by the Spirit into thirty years of wilderness preaching alone. She received no salary. She was dependent on charity and kindness for shelter and food. "Certain poverty, strenuous travel, broken health, exhausting pace: these were the rigors that defined iterant life, and for thirty years, Lee lived with them." (Florence, 45) Abiding in that broken wilderness is what made Jarena Lee both holy and human. Broken and flourishing.

As I was discerning whether to leave the church, I wrote a book about the gendered pulpit, and I thought a lot about women who gendered the pulpit in the direction of justice. I always came back to Jarena Lee. Evoking a sense of movement, as though she is walking right off the canvas, and surrounded by shades of green that covered the trails she walked from pulpit to pulpit, Lee's heart proclaims the Word:

> *Walking until she could walk no more,*
> *She preached,*
> *Her heart beating God's love*
> *For all her sisters.*

When our feet grow weary and our voices shake, when gendering the pulpit overwhelms us and we fear we cannot go on, let us remember the mighty courage of Jarena Lee. When we gender the pulpit in the direction of justice, we ordain her spirit with gratitude for the many miles she walked and the countless sermons she preached. And it was strange to me, as I straightened her icon on the pop-up's canvas awning, that my heart kept leading me back to Jarena Lee. She left it all to follow God's call to preach. I was leaving it all to follow the beckoning out of the pulpit. We would both live simply, walk miles among the trees, and proclaim liberation. We both tried standing in someone else's life, and it hadn't worked. But for different reasons. Because her call was distinctly and profoundly articulated as a call from God. With the privilege she could never claim—ordination— I was walking away from that calling and wondering if there even was a God doing the calling in the first place.

Leaving God's grace behind, I set off in search of the grace of the world, intent on lending a helping hand to all the other women scrambling over the garden's walls. Lilith and Jarena offered us courage that final night as we said goodbye to the hundred-year-old home that welcomed our child into the world, and they remained with us, tucked into a green plastic bin wedged between sleeping bags and a pack n play. The next morning, we would wake up and everything would change.

To queer the American dream, one simply must have courage. Lilith and Jarena Lee taught me this. In Lilith's case, the courage she had to leave Eden—the only place she had ever known—in search of liberation is what gave me the final boost to leave a church that was destroying my soul. It

28

was as though I could see her reaching over the stone wall closing in on me and grasping my trembling hand. "Have courage, sister. You can do this," she whispered as I began to climb, slip, cry, muster courage, and try again. Lilith had the courage to leave, walking away from what was oppressing her. With Lilith's hand in mind, I walked away, too.

Jarena Lee had the courage to go, but instead of walking away, she walked toward what was calling her. And she gave me the courage to do the same. In the face of oppression difficult for ordained white women to even fathom, she preached and walked and preached some more. Without ordination. Without vocational support. Without a spouse. Without a salary. With countless churches closed to her because of her race *and* her gender. In 1811. Still, she had the courage to keep walking. Because this is what she was called to do. Though our callings differ, it is Lee who gave me the courage to walk toward a calling not yet affirmed by anyone, really. There is no ordination council for radical imagination. No synod for leaving faith. No queer canon of saints offering a benefits package, housing allowance, and retirement plan. Lee had the courage to walk toward something greater. With my hand in hers, her courage emboldened me to do the same.

As I slept that final night in the place my queer family called home, I was emboldened by the life and legend of Jarena Lee and Lilith. When I awoke the next morning, their courage would lead me onward, and life would never quite be the same.

# Chapter 1

# Integrity
## Vermont: Freya Stark and Sophia

*"It's the beckoning that counts, not the clicking latch behind you."*
*-Freya Stark*

It's June 26, 2015. I climb behind the steering wheel as Elizabeth tucks into the back with Riah, still in a rear-facing car seat. Hitched to our bumper is our life and new home. As our historic craftsman fades in the rearview mirror, I realize that everything has already changed. Not just because we sold our home and quit our jobs and left our community, but because as we drive away from all these things, the Supreme Court makes a big change, too. SCOTUS rules in favor of marriage equality.

While packing to leave, we had already made copies of our marriage license (from Maryland before North Carolina recognized the legality of our love), two separate adoption decrees because our state did not recognize us as a family when Elizabeth first adopted Riah a brief twenty months prior, and all of the other legal paperwork that we could use to "prove" the legitimacy of our family in the case of an emergency (if medical staff wouldn't permit us both to be in a hospital room with our child, for example). With those files copied and stored neatly in a suitcase, everything changed for us. Now, no matter what state we visit, our family is legally recognized. And while I'd like to think that our paperwork is no longer necessary, I know that the legality of the court's decision doesn't automatically change the hearts and minds of everyone in the country.

Heteronormativity still reigns supreme. Hate crimes targeted at LGBTQ people actually increase after the court's decision. While we rejoice at the ruling, we simultaneously acknowledge that marriage is only one small step in dismantling straight supremacy. Though countless couples can now marry, receiving all the 1,000-plus legal rights and privileges therein, many still live in states that allow LGBTQs to be fired for our sexual orientation or gender identity, where housing may be denied, where hate crime protections do not include sexual orientation or gender identity, and the list could continue. Still, on this day, many queer people find themselves reveling in utter joy.

But our joy today is tempered by another event. As we rejoice at the Supreme Court's ruling, we also remember the life of the slain pastor of Mother Emanuel A.M.E., Rev. Clementa Pinckney. Pinckney had been murdered, along with eight congregants, by white supremacist Dylann Roof only days before. As we drive north, I wonder, amid the entrenched racism embedded in systems of power, and in the love spilling out of those beloved rainbow flags, how our hearts can hold both realities at once. As I find myself—like many others—alternating between tears of joy and tears of rage, I realize how often these two seemingly disparate emotions are an ever-present reality for most people and communities with intersectionally oppressed identities. If my own heart is torn between raging at the violence waged against black lives and celebrating that queer love is finally being acknowledged, I can't imagine how the hearts of my beloved queer black friends and colleagues are faring. And it's not simply in the past few weeks, but every week, every day, every moment, that those with intersectionally oppressed identities must experience the rending of hearts, the paradox of falling in love and having one's heart broken at the same time.

As I try to nuance how my own white privilege clouds my understanding and find myself grasping, longing, remembering, hoping, we drive. We wind through Virginia farmland and the New Jersey turnpike, make that blessed stop at Lake George and enter Vermont. And we find ourselves grasping, hoping, longing, and remembering at a little campsite on a small lake in the Green Mountains, these complex emotions a fitting entry into life on the road.

While popping up our camper in what will be our home for the next three months, I think about how many founding feminists proclaimed: the personal is political. As queer women and as a queer little family, our very lives are dubbed "social issues." The country votes on whether or not our family is valid. Courts legislate our bodies. The legitimacy of our love, our family, is a linchpin issue for political pundits who formulate campaigns on whether our family is an abomination. Because of the way our home state voted, I was not Riah's legal parent until about one month before we left. Now, many hours, piles of paperwork, numerous invasive interviews, and over three thousand extra dollars later, I am no longer considered a "legal stranger" living in Elizabeth and Riah's home. This is good because now our "home" is a camper nestled on the shores of Silver Lake in Vermont and not an historic craftsman in the West End. Nevertheless, it's nice to know that, after twenty months of love, diaper changes, late-night snuggles, and care, my title of "mama" carries with it the same legal weight every other parent in the country has.

The emotions feel big for all three of us those early days in Vermont. Between teaching multiple classes, finishing a book project, selling the house, selling a car, packing, and preparing to take a toddler—and our myriad belongings—on an eighteen-month adventure, there wasn't time to process the emotions tied to any of the aforementioned events. "How do you feel about selling your car?" I'd ask Elizabeth. "I'll let you know in mid-July," she'd respond. Replace the object of the question with the house, the dining set we painted when we first began dating, about forty boxes of books, or any of the other material things we left behind, and the response was typically the same. Now it's July, we're in Vermont, and it's time to finally address those untouched emotions.

We fill those first few days paddling the canoe, hiking, trail running, and discovering both raspberries and chanterelle mushrooms surrounding our campsite. Whatever the emotions may be, we are following the beckoning, striding in the footsteps of the intrepid Freya Stark, as her heart calls to us from that green plastic bin that had yet to be opened.

**In Her Footsteps.**

After years of having my mind mired in the esoteric quandaries of the academy and the heart-yearnings of ministry, I needed an outlet, an escape. And when I couldn't literally escape to some beautiful far-flung land via travel, I found my freedom nestled up with a good travel memoir. Travel essays, memoirs of finding oneself in another land, became my way of wandering, wondering, and learning about the world. Travelations.

Along the way I decided to support feminist and women travel writers. Over and over, I found these thoughtful writers referring back to one person, the pioneer of women's travel, the founder of this far-flung freedom. Her name was Freya Stark. Years before the plan to travel full-time hatched, I began researching her life, reading *The Passionate Nomad*, and some of her many writings based on her travels all over the world.

Born in Paris in 1893, she was one of the first European women to travel and write about the Middle East, adding Arabic and Persian to the English, French, Italian, and Latin she already knew. There are tales of her riding camels through rebel territory, taking refuge in Bedouin camps, diving into shark-infested waters off the coast of Turkey simply because the water called to her and was too beautiful to avoid immersion, or in her old age (she lived to 100), driving wildly in her hand-crafted "camper" through the Italian countryside. She lived boldly, going where few women had gone. She lived wildly, caring little about the restraints of decorum. She claimed, "It is the beckoning that counts, not the clicking latch behind you." It's no wonder that she inspired and empowered the many women travel writers that have followed in her fearless footsteps.

She also asserted, "There can be no happiness if the things we believe in are different from the things we do." Integrity. Part of our leaving it all was to try and live more in line with our beliefs, for the things we do to be the same as the things we believe. Therein lies happiness, according to Stark. I never found the courage to paint her until we began planning to leave. Though I've always tried to follow the beckoning and to "do" the things I "believe," I held back, concerned about propriety, financial responsibility, career aspirations, that clicking latch of adulthood, parenthood, a mortgage, and all the other excuses I could muster. Years after finding Freya, I decided to follow her and, in so doing, invoke her spirit into the canon of Holy Women Icons sainthood. With the courage to paint her finally a reality, I situated this holy woman amidst the far-flung places she loved so deeply. With oceans, mountains, rivers, deserts, and a starlit sky surrounding her, Freya's brave heart cries out to us:

> *With heart and mind*
> *Open to wonder,*
> *She followed the beckoning*
> *No matter the cost…*

Still so early in our own journey, I have no idea what the costs may be. At this point, we still haven't found a place to bathe, so the primary cost is the funky smell wafting from the pop-up camper, whom we aptly named Freya. The benefits are so far outweighing the costs, our hearts tethered to the ways our dream is manifesting in real time. Whatever those costs may be, Stark has taught us to have integrity, remaining faithful to the calling within, even if it's wild, unexpected, challenging, and possibly, a bit queer.

**Wonder.**

In addition to integrity, one of the many virtues we value most as a family is wonder. And instilling this value in Riah is incredibly important to us. Living full-time in the woods is an excellent way to embrace wonder. And Freya Stark's wanderings certainly evoke wonder, too. During our first week in the Green Mountain National Forest, wonder manifests as we hear a moose call—*moosamaloo*—during a stunning hike along the ridge overlooking Silver Lake. Each night, we take turns reading to Riah and tucking him in as the other mom takes the ten-minute steep hike up to Lenny's Lookout where the suns set over Lake Dunmore. As a sweaty, steep trail run draws to a close, I strip down on my way to the water, Campsuds in my filthy grasp, and bathe among the most enormous tadpoles I've ever seen. Seriously, they look like fish they're so big. For me, Silver Lake is fast becoming my family's Walden Pond as wonder surrounds, envelopes, engages us.

And we're seeing it in Riah, too. When we drove our camper out of North Carolina only ten days ago, Riah could only say about eight words. Within a week in the woods, it's as though his language has exploded. A vibrant orange newt scuttles by. He points and says, "newt." But, hands down, the most adorable development has to be his embrace of raspberries. I joked for months that we would find ourselves sheltered among patches of raspberries and blackberries with chanterelle mushrooms just around the corner. Well, months of joking have become a reality. Surrounding our camper, and throughout the entire campground, are countless raspberries with blackberries waiting in the wings to blossom. Only five miles up the dirt road are 35 acres of wild blueberries with the most stunning views of the mountains. Needless to say, Riah is getting his 3-4 servings of daily fruit.

When we first spotted raspberries, they weren't quite ripe, so I would call to them on walks with Riah, in the same manner one would call for a pet. Pitched high I called, "Raspberries, raspberries, where are you?" Upon finally finding one ripe enough to eat, I gasp, point, and let Riah pick and eat. He loves it and began to copy. "Baberry, baberry," he intones in the same sing-song pitch. When he finds a ripe one, he gasps in wonder, picks, eats, and proclaims loudly, "Mmmmm." Wonder, indeed. Working on "thank you" after eating, his cadence and pitch is spot on, but like many

34

toddlers, the "th" still sounds more like a "t." "Tank too," he proclaims with raspberry breath. Wonder. Integrity. And gratitude, too.

**Camping.**

This wonder and the stench of not bathing accompanies us on our first visit into the town of Middlebury. On our day off, we drive half an hour on a dirt road and turn toward town to hit the Farmer Market and search for showers and drinking water. Laden with three enormous water jugs, two loads of laundry, and epic pit stains, we meander the market, filling our basket with fresh pole beans in three different colors, corn, candy cane beets, and newly discovered cucamelons, an adorable cucumber that looks like a tiny watermelon. At the laundromat, I ask the owner if she can recommend a place to take a shower. She looks at my family with equal parts pity and horror. Despite growing up in a working poor family and living well below the poverty line, I never lacked for a place to clean myself. I realize, in that moment at the laundromat with the owner looking at my family in disgust, that she thinks we are homeless. Without thinking about the privilege that it entails, I quickly respond, "We're camping."

She immediately warms, suggesting we inquire at the co-op, and asking Riah if he liked sleeping under the stars. We stop at a gas station to ask the attendant if they have a hose where we can fill up water. He gives us the same look. "We're camping." His face softens, "We don't have a hose, but you're welcome to use the sink out back." He understood. Understood what, exactly? I've come to find that those two little words—"we're camping"—serve to signal our privilege to other people and put them at ease. We're stinky and dirty because we're living in the woods. We're not...poor. We're not...homeless. You don't have to feel uncomfortable around us.

As we've left the comforts of running water and air conditioning and clean clothes, people's perceptions of us have changed. They look at us more warily. They're less friendly. We've been experiencing, to an infinitesimal degree, the social and psychological toll that actual poor or unhoused people face every day.

But we do not feel the same economic toll. We retain our class privilege. We have money in the bank. We can pay our bills. We have a car. We can buy all the food we want. We can pay our medical bills. If we wanted, we could get a hotel room and take long, hot showers.

We can also utter that short phrase—"we're camping." We can correct people's perceptions of us. We can get them to see our humanity again.

Our family is spending eighteen months in the woods because we have the economic privilege to be able to do so. In discussing this under the star swathed sky while brushing our teeth, my ethicist of a wife brings up unconscious biases, and we talk of the personal transformation our family is already undergoing, but how it simply must lead to collective transformation. Collective liberation that addresses egregious inequality in this country. And our dreams for our little family expand to encompass our dreams for humanity. Access to education and healthcare. Dismantling the prison industrial complex. Raising the minimum wage. Feeding people healthy, delicious, whole foods. Universal basic income. Creating a world where every person can be inspired by their surroundings. Where everyone can brush their teeth under the star dabbled night. This is a social transformation. In many ways, it's much of what Freya Stark dreamed under star speckled skies.

After a week, the wonder doesn't wear off, and we finally find a place to bathe! There's an adorable inn five miles away, and the owner welcomes our family with open arms. After the initial awkward conversations about where our husbands are, and then upon realizing we're a family asking, "so, who is the real mom?" we're offered freshly baked cookies. Then, glory of glories, we can fill our water tanks and take a blessedly beautiful hot outdoor shower. The hot showers are on the back of a barn with a stunning view of a flower meadow in the foreground and the rolling Green Mountains in the background. The three of us wash away a week's worth of sweat, dirt, and lake water until Riah makes an escape, tearing through the fields buck naked, Elizabeth and I struggling to tie towels fast enough to chase him into the wilderness without flashing the inn owner who has shown us such hospitality.

Amidst the beauty, the amazing hikes, the utter joy I find paddling our enormous canoe out to the middle of the lake and cozying up in its belly with a book in the sunshine, and the abundant berry supply, we do, indeed, work. Of course, we have our own work—writing, art, online teaching— but we also have a few responsibilities as campground hosts. Though small, I find much of our work meaningfully humorous. Basically, we answer questions, replace toilet paper in pit toilets, and keep the campgrounds clean. This entails picking up everyone's trash, which is a sad commentary on humanity, since all the signs clearly state that hikers need to pack their rubbish in and out of the trail. Our training manual suggests eight weeks of back strengthening in order to keep up with the intense labor. We have yet to find it so intense. Lucky us.

Ever the lover of efficiency, I learn to double my trash and toilet duties (pun totally intended) with trail running. With a backpack full of toilet paper, a trash bag, and one work glove, I set out for a good four mile run along the trails. On the run out, I dash into each unoccupied campsite, checking for trash and making a mental note of where I need to stop on the way back. As I claber through the woods with my toilet-paper-laden backpack strapped snuggly to my sweating back, I feel like nothing short of an Olympic hurdler as I leap over roots, rocks, giant puddles, and small streams, a look of sheer determination across my face, my bright purple trail running shoes a blaze of glory flying by the chipmunks and woodchucks cheering me onward. In reality, I know I actually look like a nearly 34-year-old mom wearing a backpack full of toilet paper barely breaking a ten minute-mile-pace wearing the most ethically-sourced trail running shoes I could afford (bright purple was the only color available), a look of sheer horror spread across my face as mosquitoes splat into my mouth/eyes/everywhere, as a trash bag flaps aimlessly in the wind created by my ever-so-slow jog. I remain convinced that the chipmunks and woodchucks are still pretty impressed, if not by my running skills, at least by my efficiency.

After a week in the woods, and countless conversations with hikers passing by, I meet a couple with a vacation cabin on Lake Dunmore. Living in nearby Burlington, they holiday at Dunmore and occasionally hike to Silver Lake. As we chat, they mention that they're big folk-art collectors and encourage a visit to a museum in Middlebury. After sharing that I paint folk-feminist icons, they insist on seeing my work. Photos on my phone aren't enough for them, so we drag out the giant green bin of paintings from the camper, as the hearts of the women within pulsed to life. Fifteen icons spread across the picnic table, and the couple select two. "We'll buy these," they implore. I'm both shocked and delighted at the random pop-up art show among the birch trees that has resulted in two sales. The integrity of Freya Stark reminds me, in those moments unpacking canvases featuring revolutionary women, that I am following what I have been called to do, and that affirmations of living into this calling will show up in the unlikeliest places. If it takes a picnic table covered in colorful folk-feminist iconography in rural Vermont for me to know that I'm remaining true to myself, I'll take it.

## Mosquitoes

After about ten days in the wilderness, a tiny bit of the wonder begins to wear off. I try not to be a whiner. I really do. This life we're living is pretty wonderful. We're in a beautiful National Forest. We eat delicious food. We get to hike, canoe, swim, and run on trails every day. We have a sweet little toddler who is adventurous and funny, with an affinity for laughter, raspberries, dirt, and twirls. I love my wife. I'm healthy and happy and doing this thing—this eighteen months of volunteer travel discernment—that we've been hoping and dreaming and planning for all this time. Hear this. I am grateful. And privileged. And lucky. Truly.

But these damn mosquitoes.
There are so many of them. After spending over fifty dollars—yes, you read that correctly—on various mosquito repellents, we've finally found one safe and natural enough for Riah's baby soft skin, yet aggressive enough to ward off those bloodsucking beasts swarming around his little blond head.

"They should be getting better any day now," Vermonters tells us.
"The mosquitoes are usually gone by this time of year," regular Silver Lake hikers inform us. "I've never seen them this bad," mud-soaked mountain bikers insist.
Vermont has had more rain this summer than in the past 130 years. 130 years! June was the hottest June on record for the entire planet; I'm so glad climate change isn't real (insert side eye). The mosquitoes aren't bad three miles up the road, or on other hikes, or in town. They just swarm around Silver Lake and our camper and our toddler's poor little noggin. Seriously.

As vegan pacifists, there are certain values, virtues, principles by which we try to abide. Like the ethical systems of all people trying hard to be good, sometimes we fall short. But these damn mosquitoes are killing me. We're a little vegan family, for example. Don't worry, we haven't been tempted to *eat* the mosquitoes. But an obvious undergirding principle of veganism is not killing things, like animals, often even bugs. I've been known to catch a spider, even a gross roach (tucked carefully between a cup and a box and not near my hands, of course), and to rush outside flinging them wildly, yet lovingly, into the grass while shouting, "You're free!"

Elizabeth made a non-violent trap to catch fruit flies without killing them, for crying out loud. It's not really in me to kill something, even a bug, when given the choice. And I'm a pacifist, which is closely linked to my veganism. Do no harm. Try to leave things better and more beautiful than you found them, and if you can't, at least let them live. Life is valuable, worthwhile and meaningful, even if it's small, unseen, or seemingly insignificant to me. Even if it's mangy or gross or unwanted. Life is valuable. I want to respect and honor that.

And yet in recent days you could have found me, the vegan pacifist, clenched fist flying toward the canvas walls of the camper, while shouting, "Die mother fucker!" and crushing the life of a helpless mosquito, blood now splattering across the canvas and onto my knuckles. "That was quite out of character for you," I would think to myself.

It didn't start quite so violently. It began with essential oils, which actually smelled quite nice. And the mosquitoes nibbled Riah's neck and legs. It progressed to swatting and a "natural" bug spray. And the mosquitoes attacked the poor little dude's forehead. I'd say, "Sorry mosquito," while uttering a little prayer of gratitude for the bug's short life as I squashed it in a washcloth. I tried to be nice. I tried to follow my principles. I really did. But no matter how many times Elizabeth swatted and said, "Don't you bite my baby," they just wouldn't listen.

So, we kill. Ruthlessly, and sometimes with glee. Now there are at least six blood stains on the inside canvas of the camper, and the carcasses and various severed limbs of slain mosquitoes can be found throughout our belongings. We do a thorough squashing each night before bed as we literally hunt for any bloodsuckers that found their way inside and render their bodies lifeless in a washcloth specifically set aside for killing mosquitoes. Really. The washcloth isn't for washing dishes, or counters, or bodies; it isn't for wiping up spills. The sole purpose of said washcloth is the utter annihilation of mosquitoes who happen to fly into the confines of our living space. For them, it is not a living space. It is a dying space. Our camper is a mosquito graveyard. I suppose I'm more of a situational ethicist than I thought. I'll set the spiders and non-biting bugs free, but the mosquitoes must die. Integrity? Freya wonders.

## Visitations

Just as the mosquitoes finally begin to fade, my father arrives for a weeklong visit. Recently retired, he's on his own epic journey, riding a motorcycle from Georgia through Canada, stopping to camp with us along the way. Though we've had our share difficulties in our relationship, my dad is a dedicated grandparent with a wanderlust only matched by his camper-towing daughter. After one night of sleeping in his pitched tent right next to our camper, we inform him we simply must have a barrier of trees to block the roar of his snores that raged through the canvas of the pop-up, keeping us awake throughout the night. Content knowing his snores would likely keep the bears away, he scoots into a grove of trees not too far from us. As an incredibly early riser, he taps on the camper door each morning when he hears Riah wake up so the two road weary moms can sleep a little more. Wonder and gratitude. Again.

Not only does dad's visit entail a little extra sleep, it also means that Elizabeth and I get to go on an actual date. Itching to take longer and more strenuous hikes than we can handle with Riah in a pack, we set off to explore Rattlesnake Cliffs. Fortunately, Vermont doesn't actually have rattlesnakes, or any poisonous snakes. This was one of the first questions I asked Ranger Dave—who doubles as a reggae DJ on weekends—during orientation because my fear of snakes is only second to my fear of failure. I loathe them. During our first wonder-filled week at Silver Lake, however, I encountered more snakes that I could count. I started counting but stopped when I passed twenty-five.

During my first encounter, our little family was hanging hand-washed laundry on a line between two birch trees when the completely innocuous black garden snake slithered in my line of vision. I screamed in a manner matched only by a very frightened Julia Child and did what I have dubbed "an exaggerated high-knee Broadway run" for at least one hundred yards. After the fact, I realized that such a response to a small, harmless snake probably doesn't set the best example for my young child. So, I began working on my fear of snakes. Though I still screamed and ran when one slithered into the pit toilet while I was doing my business, I developed a pretty solid tolerance of these harmless little snakes. In fact, about two weeks after the exaggerated high-knee Broadway run incident, I was doing sit-ups on my yoga mat in a patch of grass when a snake slithered only inches away. I paused with contracted abs, acknowledged the snake, and kept on crunching.

By the time Elizabeth and I embark on our blessed hiking date, I feel pretty confident that, despite its name, Ranger Dave wouldn't steer me wrong in telling me there were no rattlesnakes in Vermont. So, Elizabeth and I hike. Together. Sometimes even holding hands. Without having to repeatedly pass snacks to our toddler. Or play the alphabet game. Or the "what sound does this animal make" game. Or without twenty-five extra wiggly pounds on our backs. It is glorious and sweaty and beautiful. And a week later, we'll both get to take a hot shower, drive into town, and eat dinner together. Without having to feed anyone else. Or worry about flying food. Or bears. I'll even wear a dress.

We meet campers, clean pit toilets, redirect lost hikers, and shovel out fire pits. After helping a family's injured older father back to the trailhead, the family returns a week later with maple syrup sugared from trees in their own yard. A few days later, a family who just didn't want to pack out all their leftover food delivers more freshly made maple syrup, along with bags of trail mix and popcorn. Inspired by the raspberry and blueberry surroundings and the gifted maple syrup, Elizabeth begins making the most delicious blueberry pancakes. It is marvelous.

**Herstory**

The marvel continues after dad leaves, as the blackberries begin to ripen and wild apples form on trees surrounding us, and we create a rhythm around the lake. After completing my trail running chores, and once I'm thoroughly drenched in sweat, I grab a book and push our enormous 15-foot canoe into the frigid waters of Silver Lake. With a smile that has yet to wipe off my face, I paddle fiercely. I'm typically the only person on the lake.

It's a steep mile hike to the lake from the trailhead, and we're the only ones "living" here for the summer, so my giant green canoe ripples the silvery waters in solitude. Once I find the right spot, I stuff my life vest behind my head, strip naked in the sun, and cozy down into the belly of the canoe, book in hand, goofy grin still spread across my flushed face. In the warmth of the sun, I read. In the belly of the canoe, I drift into the history of the lake, the unwritten annals lapping alongside my rocking boat, the portions on record filling the book in my sun-warmed hands.

The author who wrote the history of Silver Lake, William Powers, had hiked up with several autographed copies in his rucksack only days after our arrival. He's a nice man who wrote a nice book. There's nothing like reading about the history of a place while in the place. Hear me say this clearly: there's nothing wrong with the nice book this nice man wrote. The stories of Frank Chandler feeling a call from God to build a place for religious camp meetings along Silver Lake's shores are fascinating, an interesting part of the history of camp meetings that filled the Awakenings throughout the United States. But as I read about Frank Chandler and the various men who the logged roads hikers now hike and built the buildings that haven't existed for years due to fire, I can't help but notice who was missing.

Sure, Frank Chandler was married, and his wife's name is included in the history of Silver Lake. So are the wives and daughters of various other men important to this place's history. The history book was written with copious notes, citations based on court records, marriage licenses, property purchases, taxes, and every other legal document on record. It's the way history is usually remembered, recorded, and recounted.

Though I know semantics are incredibly important, that our language has power, and that subverting, shifting, gendering, and queering such language is a vital part of effecting change, I'll be honest in saying that I've never really been one to use the term "herstory" instead of "history." I'm not quite sure why. Perhaps it seemed a bit trite. Maybe because its etymological history has little to do with the semantic shift. Or it's possible that internalized sexism still exists within me in forgotten places, in the places that only show up when you're curled into the belly of a canoe, floating in the belly of the Green Mountains, womblike, cradling, and naked in the sun.

But as I read and float and learn about the religious fervor of all these white men, I can't help but think about how I'm reading precisely what religious history—all history—is about: men's religious fervor. There is no record of what Frank Chandler's wife did at the religious camp meetings on Silver Lake because her perspective didn't matter. We do get to read her name, though: Ellen Alden Chandler. As I completed this book, my eyelids heavy and my hands sun-kissed, it was true that, not only had I missed any stories about Ellen Alden Chandler, but the stories of the countless Abenaki women who had canoed, splashed, birthed, loved, laughed, and died in these chilly waters were not even mentioned. I say this, not to critique the author of the history of this small lake in the small state of Vermont, but to name how illustrative this "'his'story" is embedded in the history of every place. *Her* voices are missing. The sacred voices of women are missing. And the sacred voices of women of color, in particular, are missing altogether. What is the "herstory" of Silver Lake?

I'm convinced Freya would know how to find out, so I take up this question during children's story time at the public library, perusing the annals, finding little about the Abenaki women driven from this place my family is calling home for the summer. What are their stories? We share what stories we can find with our families when they visited. Next comes Elizabeth's mom and her husband who paddled my canoe in search of loons.

**Mishaps**

My canoe has developed a small problem that sometimes prevents my naked sunshine reading. It appears that a snake or two enjoys sleeping under the overturned canoe when it is on the shore. I learned this the hard way a few days ago when I flipped the canoe and two snakes came rushing toward me. No matter how much work I'd done to assuage my fears, I couldn't help but scream and hike up my knees.

Since the initial shock, however, I have developed a seemingly fail-proof method to avoid snake attacks upon flipping the canoe. I simply beat the canoe with paddles while singing loudly like a wild woman before flipping it. Inevitably, the snakes will slither in the opposite direction, afraid of the oar-laden woman wailing like a banshee. Though it feels fool-proof, I just can't risk the naked read in the canoe's belly anymore. I am fearful that a snake might brave my raucous entry by stowing away in a storage compartment, only to slither out and greet me eye-to-eye with a parseltongue greeting, "Hello, Eve."

Fortunately, this is never a problem for Elizabeth's parents. During their visit, they treat us to one night in a hotel where they are staying in town. This means we have access to two luxuries: running water and WiFi. Embarrassingly, we had quickly realized that losing access to the latter was even harder than the former. I suppose that's the world we live in now. Fortunately, the kind people at the nearby inn had welcomed us to use their

WiFi as long as we weren't interrupting guests. Still, this entailed hiking five miles with a laptop and hunkering in the shadows outside the Inn hoping for a signal strong enough to download a writing contract, or respond to a lingering email that needed more attention and typing skills than my phone could offer. This was one of the challenging downfalls of life in the woods while still working. Doing ordinary things, like printing and signing a contract for a writing gig, banking, or downloading anything usually involved a 45-minute drive to town, remembering everything that needed to be accomplished online, and waiting for access at the public library. A task that would have taken three minutes in our "ordinary" life now took three hours. As a lover of efficiency, this nagged at me.

So, such luxuries in a hotel are a welcome reprieve for one night. Though we relish the wonder of the woods, it's nice to sleep in a regular bed and use a regular toilet. This specific luxury is particularly elusive only days after our visit to the hotel. On our drive back to the camper, a baby bear runs in front of the car. Where there's a baby bear, a mama bear is not far behind. I drive tentatively forward, keeping on eye on the same dirt road Elizabeth and I run on almost every day, grateful the bear had never crossed our path while on foot, and reminding myself to carry bear spray on my next run.

We arrive back at the camper just in time for dinner and bed, when the clouds erupt, rain battering Little Freya's canvas cover. Later that rainy evening, as we snuggle in bed, a feeling comes over me. It's a feeling almost everyone has almost every day, but in this particular moment, it is one of the most unwelcome feelings I've had in a long time. I have to poop. Now, we've developed a pretty solid potty strategy while living without a toilet or running water. There are pit toilets, but you have to hike to them. And they're *pit toilets*. No matter how well we sweep them or restock their toilet paper, nothing makes them less of a pit full of shit and piss. So, unless it was an emergency, we avoid using them, preferring to just go outside or use the tiny toilet in the camper instead. Except for poops. These are things you learn to discuss without shame while living this way, apparently.

The pop-up camper has a little toilet that flushes into what is best described as a plastic suitcase. A locking mechanism allows you to safely secure the hole into the toilet when you pull said plastic suitcase, now heavy with piss, out of the camper. Emptying this little suitcase is my responsibility, though I can't quite remember why. About once a week, I have to lock the mechanism, muscle the plastic suitcase out of the camper's side compartment, and wheel it to one of the pit toilets to drain out all our pee. With one caveat: This is a chore I refuse if either of us has pooped in it. Hence, our treks to poop in the pit toilets.

Thinking the suitcase-hauling task is hilarious, Elizabeth always sings, "my baby takes the morning train," as I clamor down the trail toward the pit toilet, hauling a suitcase full of urine behind me. I never have figured out why she selected this particular song to add a musical flair to such a gross task, but not one suitcase-emptying goes by without her serenade. Her melodies are always accompanied by a little shimmying dance, and though I love my wife very much, this only adds to the humor because she is not the most skilled dancer.

So, as the downpour continues after our bear sighting, I just can't fight the urge to poop any longer. I'm not going to hike to the pit toilet in the pouring rain at 10pm, especially after seeing a bear. I don't just want to go in the woods because that wouldn't stop the rain or the bear. And I won't poop in our camper toilet because I'm responsible for emptying it. This whole living in the woods thing has really gotten me into a pickle. With Elizabeth the ethicist aiding me in my dilemma, we determine the best course of action is to put a plastic bag inside the toilet, poop in the bag, and then gently place the tied-up bag outside the door, and dispose of it properly in morning. This is precisely what we do with Riah's nighttime poop diapers. Then, I'm faced with yet another dilemma.

You see, a pop-up camper has no privacy. The toilet is just out in the open for everyone to see, about two feet from the stove. Now, after a decade-long relationship, Elizabeth and I pee in front of each other all the time. No big deal. But pooping is another story. So, I convince Elizabeth to hide under the covers, not to peek, and to speak of this to no one. And then I poop in the bag.

As I tie the bag and place it outside the camper door, I remember my dad's quandary when he accompanied me on my chores one afternoon. My dad playfully questioned my life choices. "Ang, did you ever think that you'd finish a PhD only to clean out pit toilets? I didn't finish high school, and I've done some nasty jobs in my day, but never a pit toilet." Intended as silly jab, his comment actually got me thinking a lot about economic and educational privilege. Why shouldn't I clean a pit toilet? Is there something about having access to higher education that should exempt me from

45

cleaning my own waste? This is the American dream, right? Live here. Get an education. Make money. Avoid cleaning your own waste. Avoid getting your hands dirty. By no means do I want to sweep pit toilets for the rest of my life, but this life I'm leading is one I created, and one for which I am profoundly grateful. Even if it occasionally involves pooping in a bag.

**Birthday.**

As July fades into August, my mom and aunt come to visit. Almost every year for thirty-four years, the three of us have celebrated our birthdays together. The Leo Party, we call it. So, mom and Auntie Margaret scope out our digs at the campground and then treat us to another night at a hotel. Cake and dinners out, waterfalls and covered bridges, Farmer Market and maple candies fill our day until my queer little family returns to our camper once again just in time to celebrate my 34th birthday.

It's usually pretty quiet around here. Volunteering in a National Forest with a backpack-in campground tends toward tranquility in the evenings, with its stunning sunsets, starry nights, and tired campers. At night we hear crickets, loons, owls, bullfrogs, and the occasional moose. Every once in a while there will be some loud campers, but it doesn't last too long. And then there's tonight: Friday, August 21.

6:45pm
The evening is supposed to be fabulous in every way, seeing as how it is my birthday eve. Elizabeth is in the camper cooking up some delicious vegan rice crispy treats to kick off the celebration. I'm playing outside with Riah. A group of rambunctious hikers ascends the hill, we all wave and continue to play. They walk toward the lake, as most hikers do. I'm not paying much attention, but I hear "canoe," "sticks," "maybe we should ask the hosts," and "nah." Uh oh.

I'm not really one for confrontation, but I don't want anyone stealing my canoe or trying to paddle it with sticks. I'm actually happy to loan it to pretty much anyone who asks, along with paddles, life vests, and a long explanation about snake prevention. I hear some ruckus and a splash. Riah follows me in their direction. Since I'm not a confrontation fan, I don't really know what to say when I see 5 people inside my green canoe with sticks in their hands, their 2 additional friends pushing the laden ark into the frigid waters.

"That's mine," I utter.

"Oh. We didn't know. We just assumed it was an abandoned canoe," they say as they scramble out.

"It's not a big deal, but if you want to use it, you can just ask and I'll loan you the paddles," I respond, a little annoyed.

"We wouldn't want to inconvenience you. We couldn't possibly," they claim as they walk away, stick-paddles in hand.

"Mine," Riah declares.

11:10pm
Riah is asleep. We're in bed, beginning to doze when we hear rumbling outside, and a flash of light illuminates the camper. It's a large truck driving down the road. Our "road" is a gated hiking path. The only cars permitted to drive on it are those with 4-wheel drive and keys to the lock—Forestry Service, Power Company, Sherriff—and all these groups only drive the roads during the day. The truck parks just in front of the camper and slams the door. It's the police. Lovely. I head outside to scope out the situation. If there's an escaped murderer or ravage bear on the loose, I think we may prefer to go into town and stay in a hotel again. It turns out that some backpacker got lost and called 911. The reception was bad and all they heard was "lost" and "Silver Lake." The officer asks me if I've seen a 50-something-year-old woman named Linda from New Hampshire. They traced the cell number to find this information and were trying to find her.

Alas, there are no 50-something-year-old women named Linda from New Hampshire staying in our camper. So, the officer continues his search, which includes shining flashlights in backpackers' tents and asking if they are lost women named Linda from New Hampshire. I don't find this to be the most useful tactic, seeing as how lost people generally don't sleep in their found tents, but I don't offer any alternative suggestions and instead retire to enjoy my last evening of sleep as a 33-year old.

Sometime between 11:10pm and 2:20am
The loons and owls are going wild. They must know something is amok.

2:20am
Riah, Elizabeth, and I are all asleep. A rambunctious group of hikers bounds up the hill with shining flashlights, loud guffaws, and a lot of yelling. It's not a full moon or anything; I have no idea why they are doing a

47

long, steep hike in the middle of the night and I certainly am not interested in them waking up my toddler with all their hollering. I throw open the camper door, clad in disheveled pjs.

"Sssshhhhhhhhh," I hiss, hoping this "calming" noise won't wake Riah.
They immediately get quiet. I don't think they intended to be rude and probably didn't realize there were two moms and a toddler sleeping next to the lake where they were likely going skinny dipping. I consider warning them about the enormous tadpoles and snakes, but decide to let them risk it.

2:45am
We are awakened by a loud banging. Someone is knocking on our camper door. I try not to overreact or jump to conclusions, but even as a hardcore radical feminist, I'm still a little nervous since we're two little women living in the middle of the woods with our toddler and nothing but a screen protecting us from the person banging on our door at 2:45am.
"Ssssshhhhhhhh," is my immediate reaction. Don't wake the damn baby!
I jump out of bed and stand in front of the door and whisper.
"We have a sleeping baby. Please be quiet," though it crosses my mind to say, "Are you a 50-something-year-old woman named Linda from New Hampshire?"
"I'm sorry," a manly sounding voice responds, "My flashlight is out of batteries and I can't find my camp. Can you help?"
I rustle around for AAA batteries and step outside to greet a young man in shorts and t-shirt with 3 empty Gatorade bottles and a dark flashlight.
"Did you call the police earlier?" I ask him.
"Yes. They found me."
I am puzzled as to why he is standing at my door after being found.
"Are you a 50-something-year-old woman named Linda from New Hampshire?" I ask him.
"What?"
I repeat the question, adding that the police told me that was the description of the person they were looking for.
"Oh, that's my mom," he tells me. Family cell phone plan.

He then informs me that he can't find his camp. When I ask him what number camp he's staying in, I learn that he decided it would be more fun to camp in a random spot off a trail, and he can't remember which trail it is. This is not allowed, but I figured that didn't really matter at the moment. I give him my super bright lantern, ask him to return it in the morning, and wish him luck.

Sometime between 2:45am and 4:15am
The loons and owls are going wild. They must know something is amok. I hear a moose in the distance, "Moosamaloo!"
4:15am
Said noisy hikers tromp back by the camper. They aren't super noisy, but I have never really gotten back to sleep and can hear their footsteps and whispers. I appreciate that they remembered to be quiet on their return trip.
6:15am
Riah wakes up. This kinda sucks for Elizabeth because it's my birthday and I get to sleep in. They go off on an adventure while I sleep until 8am.

8:30am
Someone is banging on the door. It's the 20-something guy with my lantern. He found his camp and shares both his gratitude and embarrassment.

It seems that every possible thing that could be noisy and out of the ordinary managed to happen in one night. Weird. But now it's my birthday and I got to sleep in and I'm ready for a fabulous day. After some writing I head off to teach my Saturday morning yoga class by the lake. I'm greeted by a super cool family who backpacked in and recently moved to Vermont from Alaska. We do yoga together overlooking Silver Lake, surrounded by birch trees, saluting a warm sun, and opening our hearts up toward a bright blue sky. Life is good. As we rise from final shivasana and chat, Elizabeth and Riah greet me with birthday hugs. Riah and I play on the beach with the cool family and their dogs while Elizabeth goes back to the camper to make a surprise brunch.

Vegan French toast with Vermont maple peanut butter, Vermont maple syrup, and wild apples and berries from around the forest. A set of 3 and 4 yellow candles flame atop my serving. I make a wish and chow down. During Riah's nap I take a beautiful, long, steep trail run to a stunning waterfall and return to hop into my canoe for a quick paddle. Fortunately, neither rowdy hikers with sticks nor snakes were awaiting me. After a "lake bath," we put on our "going into town clothes" and head to Middlebury for some delicious curry.

When we return, Elizabeth puts Riah to bed as I hike up to Lenny's Lookout to take in the sunset. It has been pretty much the perfect day. I think 34 is going to be a wonderful year.

I'm generally not a big fan of the word "blessing," though I'd use it to describe this day. When most people hear "blessing," they think of some Transcendent Other—usually God—blessing some people. Many claim that said God blesses them if they get a promotion or if luck is in their favor or if their favorite sports team wins or if they find a suitable mate. For me, this is bad theology. For if this God is blessing some, that means the same God is withholding blessings from others. And while I loved my French toast, I don't think some Transcendent Other was giving me a birthday blessing because of it. Nor do think some Transcendent Other is withholding blessings from those without tasty French toast, or those with no food at all. That's bad theology. But I think I'm at a place, in my 34th year, to reclaim this word: blessing. I'm not associating it with some Transcendent Other who blesses and/or curses. Rather I'm associating it with our abilities to bless others. And by bless I mean show love, compassion, empathy, joy, hope, and peace. My beautiful little family showed me love, joy, compassion, laughter, thoughtfulness, and peace on my birthday. They blessed me. And it is because of these beautiful people in my life—the people who bless me daily—I think my 34th year is off to a pretty great start.

**Mirrors.**

The celebration continues as we welcome Elizabeth's dad and his wife as our next visitors. Not too keen on the woods, they treat us to not one, but two nights in a hotel! I haven't been this clean and rested all summer. Freshly cleansed, I stand naked in front of a foggy full-length mirror. I have just taken my first hot, indoor shower in nearly two months. There's no running water in the camper, and there are certainly no mirrors hanging from the birch trees. Sure, I can catch a glimpse of myself in the rearview mirror of my car, but this is the first time I have seen all of me—sun-kissed and mosquito-bitten—in a while. This may not seem like a big deal, and I didn't think it would be, but the absence of mirrors has had a profoundly holy impact on me this summer.

As the dirt of two months swirled down the shower drain and I savored every drop of warm water pouring endlessly over my aching body, I thought about the mirror that awaited me. I thought about how it has been almost fifteen years since I've intentionally starved myself or shoved my finger down my throat to induce calorie-purging vomit. I thought about how I weigh thirty pounds more than I did during the nadir of my eating disorder. I thought about how much grace I've offered my body over these years. The grace to grow. The grace to age. The grace to gain. The grace to work hard. The grace to accept.

I thought about the tremendous privilege my body carries: the privilege of my whiteness, the privilege of being temporarily able-bodied, thin privilege. I thought about how my white body has never feared for her life when pulled over for a traffic violation. I thought about how my body has access to do whatever she wants—climb stairs into inaccessible buildings, or mountains to stunning vistas. I thought about how I can find clothing in my size in virtually any store, how no one offers me health advice when ordering at a restaurant or diminishes my concerns at the doctor's office based on my size. I thought about racism, ableism, and fatphobia. I thought about what it means to be a queer femme body. I thought about the integrity Freya Stark has taught me, yet how my feelings often conflict with my philosophy of how bodies deserve to be treated. Feelings of shame and disgust when I want to be feeling affirmation, acceptance, even adoration for the beauty of my body.

And I thought about the eating disorder that still lives inside me, the one that sometimes rages and judges and shames no matter how much body-positivity and feministing and queering I do. I thought about the white supremacist cis-heteronormative bullshit that is thrown at my body—at all bodies—on a daily basis, that popular culture reaches me even when I'm living in the middle of the woods with misogynistic, capitalistic shouts of thigh gaps and dad bods. I thought about the paradox that dwells within me, simultaneously carrying the privilege of being white, cis, thin, and normatively abled, but also the struggle of being a queer woman with a painful history of being poor while having eating disorders.

I thought about how much religion fueled my disorder, admonishing me to "be perfect as my Heavenly Father is perfect," to "take up my cross," to "deny myself." I thought about the piety of countless medieval mystic women who were told that denying themselves any sustenance was a means of identifying with the suffering of Christ. Historians refer to this as anorexia mirabilis, or the miraculous loss of appetite (Lelwica, Starving for Salvation, 27). I thought about how mystics greatly admired, such as

51

Catherine of Sienna, struggled with disordered eating. She reportedly lived on the Eucharist alone, gave away her food to the hungry, and stuck twigs down her throat to induce vomiting. I thought about how clinicians estimate that eighty to eighty-five percent of American women—across racial and socio-economic lines—have Sub-clinical Eating Disorders (SED). SED describes individuals who are obsessed with weight and body image and is characterized by chronic under-eating, over-exercising, and binge-eating resulting from long periods of self-starvation. 80% of women think their bodies aren't good enough, worthy enough, holy enough, enough.

I thought about all these things as the water washed over my broken body. I thought about how far I had come, yet how angry I was that this disorder still dwells within. I thought about the shame I felt that, even after much work and outward declarations of body positivity, there's still a part of me that hopes every time I thrust my fist into the air in protest, it reveals a trim and sculpted tricep. How absolutely and utterly ridiculous and unfeminist is that?! It's about as ridiculous as it is true and real.

Now as I wipe the steamy mirror to reveal my body, now cleansed—purified? baptized?—I think of the immortal words of Gloria Steinem and Jane Fonda. They encourage feminists, upon looking into the mirror, to imagine that a little girl is watching and absorbing every negative thing said about your body. Would you say those things to her? Of course not. Then don't say them to yourself, either. I think about all those years of body shaming, the years my religious tradition choked and starved my self-esteem so violently. I think about how religion is used to violate the bodies of women and girls every day.

As I look into that mirror and the voices of my disorder stir within me, I take a deep breath. I breathe in grace, acceptance, and peace. And I think about how my legs—even without the notorious thigh gap—had completed a beautiful, steep, 10-mile trail run through fern fields and wildflowers earlier that week. I think about how my shoulders carried my toddler in a pack on a hike to a waterfall where he repeated his alphabet for the first time the day prior. I think about how my stomach had willingly held down almost every meal for the past fifteen years. And I think about Sophia Wisdom.

Sophia was the first Holy Woman Icon with a folk-feminist twist I ever painted. A church gallery was hosting a Lenten triptych exhibit with the theme of "The Many Faces of Jesus." I knew immediately that the face of Jesus I wanted to portray was Sophia wisdom. Sophia is the Greek feminine word for wisdom in the New Testament.

With big, open hands reaching beyond the confines of her canvas and expanding onto either side of the triptych, the wild and flowing hair of Spirit Sophia waves in Dionysian abandon, and we look into her beating heart and see ourselves, our own spirits reflected back at us. And Sophia's heart cries out to us:

> *Because she looked into the eyes of fragile humanity and saw the face of Jesus,*
> *her heart shattered at the sight of oppression and injustice…*
> *so she committed herself to a lifetime of picking up the broken pieces*
> *by standing for peace and dancing for justice…*
> *and now when she looks into the mirror,*
> *she sees the face of Jesus once again…*

The fragments in her heart are shards of mirrors. Still in front of the mirror, I think about how Sophia has accompanied me into the wilderness, nestled among her revolutionary sisters in that enormous green plastic bin. The only mirrors present with me in the forest are broken on her big, beating heart. I look into that foggy full-length mirror, and I look into the broken mirror on Sophia's heart, and I see a reflection of broken, redeemed, and resurrected humanity. I see myself, the queer feminist whose disorder will always be lurking below the surface, but who has realized the strong grace of Sophia is enough to sustain me. No matter the feelings that sometimes rage, critique, and shame, there is integrity in honoring where my body has been, and where it hopes to go. Sophia and Freya remind me of this.

With integrity and wisdom, the stench of three months, and the carcasses of countless mosquitoes, we pack up our camper to leave the Green Mountains. September is upon us, and the leaves are just beginning to change. A chill is in the air, Freya is beckoning us onward, and Sophia's grace holds us steady as we begin the slow journey to Virginia. With integrity, we go.

## Chapter 2

# Hope
# The Southeast:
# Pauli Murray and Mary

*"Hope is a song in a weary throat. Give me a song of hope and a world where I can sing it."*
*-Pauli Murray*

As we leave the Green Mountains behind and make our way south, we stop to visit Riah's remaining grandparents at their fabulous condo in Rehoboth Beach. Birth Grandma Colleen and her wife welcome us with abundant hospitality. Slippers wait by our beds, wine flows, the refrigerator is stocked with vegan food, delicious meals are shared, and they treat Riah to quite a shopping spree. These are things we cannot do without help, examples of what it means to queer family by visiting with Riah's queer paternal birth grandmothers. As we finish our visit and drive toward DC for me to lecture at American University, I have a chance to reflect on the visits with grandparents and marinate further on what it means for us to queer our family.

Between adoption, divorce, and remarriage, Riah has lucked into having eight loving grandparents, three fun uncles (and a soon-to-be aunt-in-law), two absolutely amazing birth parents, and a slew of awesome friends who are like family. We have the great privilege of having family by both choice and blood. We know this is a luxury most queer families do not have. Both experience and statistics remind us that the love and acceptance our extended family has shown is the exception and not the norm. As a pastor, I cannot tell you the number of queer congregants I know who have had parents kick them out of the house upon coming out, or who have beaten them and told them they are no longer a part of the family, or who shame them and tell them they're destined for hell.

In the LGBTQ community, family is often a tenuous, even volatile concept. Being disowned by family happens all the time. Physical violence is often a reality or concern. Sometimes parents go decades without knowing their child is queer because the fear of violence, revulsion, or exclusion is so real. Sometimes parents never know. Sometimes families are "ok," but still shame, exclude, undercut, and treat the queer person as thought their identity and/or relationship is less worthy, less real. Lying, blaming, tricking, excluding, disowning. These are often the ways queer people are treated by their "families."

In Janet Mock's stunning memoir, *Redefining Realness*, I think her statement sums up perfectly the reality for so many queer people who struggle with the notion of family:

> "I think of the hundreds of thousands of LGBTQ youth who are flung from intolerant homes, from families who reject them when they reveal themselves. Of the estimated 1.6 million homeless and runaway American youth, as many as 40 percent are LGBTQ [when LGBTQ folks actually only comprise about 10% of the overall population]. These young people are kicked out of their homes or are left with no choice but to leave because they can't be themselves (109)."

These realities make us acutely aware that what we have and what we have created as family is unique; it is something we must never take for granted. Are our families perfect? No way. Do we always agree on everything? Nope. Have there been times when our queerness has been a struggle for some of our parents? Absolutely. But here they are, making the trip to Vermont from Georgia, North Carolina, and Florida, welcoming us into their home in Delaware. Here they are with flashlights, hotel stays, babysitting, vegan marshmallows, and house slippers.

Being queer is a beautiful, revolutionary, life-changing gift. My queerness helped my father and me become closer. Our queerness has helped both of us open our eyes to the ways in which others are excluded and marginalized in society. Our queerness led an absolutely brilliant, thoughtful pregnant woman to choose us to parent her child, not in spite of our difference, but because of it. And now we are a big, loving, expanding, queer family. Queerness is often used within the LGBTQ community to mean "to transgress, to act differently than the status quo." I can think of few better ways to parent and to be a family than by transgressing the exclusionary patterns posited by society and acting differently than the status quo. Or, as the revolutionary queer theologian Marcella Althaus-Reid stated in *Indecent Theology*, "Therefore, liberationist or not, we are always called to confess and repent from normality and its policy of toleration, and we need to stop the circle of life-energy wasting process of trying to fit into that ideal heterosexual being we should be (131)." Yes, we want equal rights. But I'm not interested in heterosexual normality and gender norms bent on placing dynamically nuanced individuals into one of two confining boxes.

As I lecture on the queerness of dance in scripture at American University while the pope's visit stalls Washington to a gridlock, I feel the pushback, seminarians giving me the side eye at the thought of Judith or David or the Shulamite—characters beloved in their sacred texts—actually being queer dancers who subverted what it means to love and worship. But I also witness the resilience of some students grappling with fusing their sexuality and spirituality in creative and subversive ways. The queerness of our family, the eight grandparents, the open adoption, the words of challenge and gratitude from seminary students accompanies us as our camper chugs into rebel territory. After driving past the tenth confederate flag hampering the beauty of Southern Virginia's autumnal glory, I begin to think of the icon-activists that fill the green bin crammed in our camper's storage compartment. The heart beating loudest is Pauli Murray.

**Hope.**

Pauli Murray was a queer black woman who was raised in Durham, NC by her aunt after her parents died. She was a civil rights attorney, coining the phrase "Jane Crow" to acknowledge the role of sexism in addition to racism in Jim Crow laws. In her sixties, she became the first African American woman to be ordained as an Episcopal priest. All the while she loved women, even claiming that if she could transition from Pauli to Paul, she would, thus providing hope and holiness, not only for women, lesbians, and African Americans, but also for transgender persons.

Murray was ahead of her time in so many subversive and prophetic ways. She graduated from Hunter College, intent on attending law school so that she could work for justice for black women. In 1938, she was rejected from UNC Chapel Hill's law school because of her race and Harvard because of her gender. She even received a prestigious scholarship from Harvard when the admissions committee assumed that "Pauli" was a man's name; upon discovering that Pauli was a woman, they revoked the scholarship and admission into the law school. Undeterred, she continued to hope, and enrolled in law school at UC Berkeley. Upon finishing, she published a book, *States' Laws on Race and Color*, which was described by Thurgood Marshall as the bible for civil rights attorneys. She lost a teaching post at Cornell University because of the people who wrote her reference letters, the legendary Eleanor Roosevelt, Thurgood Marshall, and Philip Randolph, who were all dubbed too radical by the university.

Yet Murray continued working for equality, jailed for organizing desegregation on public transportation years before Rosa Parks, in addition to planning sit-ins twenty years before the famous Woolworth's protests in Greensboro. In 1965, she was the first black woman to earn a law doctorate at Yale. As a celebration, she co-founded the National Organization for Women (NOW).

After challenging the status quo in law, Murray followed her call to pursue the priesthood in her 60s. She began her studies at New York's General Theological Seminary before the Episcopal Church permitted women to become priests. In 1977, she was ordained and presided at her first Eucharist at the Chapel of the Holy Cross in Chapel Hill, NC. It was the same church where her grandmother—then enslaved—was baptized.

Throughout her career in civil rights and in the priesthood, Murray had loving, committed, and intimate relationships with women and struggled to articulate her gender identity. Throughout the 1920s and 30s she took hormone treatments as she described herself as a "man trapped in a woman's body." Today Murray may have described herself as transgender or gender queer, though such language was not readily available to her during her lifetime. She lived and loved boldly, finding the magnanimous balance between humility and pride, and working tirelessly so that all may be treated equally. When the world seemed hopeless, Murray hoped. When doors seemed to close—because of her race, gender, sexuality, or gender identity—Murray found the audacity to keep knocking.

As I painted her icon, I knew that her heart must be the largest of all, encompassing more of the canvas than her body. With a quiet resolve, she stands with her arms spread wide, embracing everyone, as her heart cries out to us:

*When her throat grew weary,*
*Her heart pulsed a song*
*Of hope, of justice, of equality,*
*Unconstrained by the binaries*
*That bind,*
*Authentically free...*

So often, people claim we've come so far. And our country has made progress since Pauli Murray lived. She couldn't legally be denied entrance into schools because of her race or gender today, but still for her sexuality. And attending virtually any school as a queer black woman is still rife with microaggressions; she'd likely be the only one, or one of the few, in most of her classes. She could be out and marry a woman if she chose since this has now been legal for a few months. She would have access to the word, "transgender," though depending on her health insurance, she may not have affordable access to meds, counseling, or gender confirmation surgery. She could still be fired or denied housing because of her sexuality or gender identity.

I wonder how she might feel driving through Southern Virginia right now. The vibrant scarlets, burnt oranges, and crisp golds erupt off trees, even amidst the endless rainfall. Yet, those flags remain intentionally placed, billowing systemic racism to all who pass. Where is Murray's hope in this place?

We arrive at our new campground, wary of how our family might be treated, drenched once again. The previous campground hosts—a retired couple with a big rig—are still present, so we have to pop up Little Freya in a different spot for a couple nights. When they leave for fall and winter in Arizona, we need to move our camper five sites over into the spot designated for volunteer campground hosts. Taking down and popping up would take about 2 hours in the rain, so we decide to risk towing the camper while open. In the drizzle, we hitch the open pop up to the rusty Explorer. Elizabeth inches forward at two miles per hour while I walk alongside with Riah perched on my hip, holding parts of the canvas in place so it won't lurch off the camper in transport. Fortunately, the rain has warded campers away, so the campground is empty. We've received enough funny looks already.

With Little Freya settled in her nook at Racoon Branch, it is time for me to bid my family farewell for the day as I drive an hour to Boone, North Carolina to hang an exhibit of my Holy Women Icons. It was supposed to be accompanied by a retreat, but it has been delayed due to flooding. The deluge theme of our travels continues. Winding through mountain roads bursting with color, I haul my green bin of icons upward, landing at a progressive, liberal congregation nestled on the edge of a holler overlooking farm country. I am wary. Church has burned me, but after conversations with their queer woman pastor, I felt this would be a good place to hang a show, lead a few retreats, preach, and trouble the waters of faithlessness once again.

With my icons covering one sanctuary wall, and candles flickering across the base, the exhibit begins to take on the feel of altar, which is fitting as we near All Saints Day and Dia de los Muertos. These paintings of revolutionary women are my offrenda, an offering of remembrance and hope. As I am hanging the last painting—of Pauli Murray, no less—the pastor brings up a group the church was considering creating: Spirituality for Non-Theists. They were in the beginning phases of discussing the role of the many atheists, agnostics, Buddhists, and non-theists in the congregation. Like John Wesley, the founder of Methodism so many years ago, my heart is strangely warmed at the mere thought of it. His heart was warmed by God's call. Mine is warmed by call away from theism. This was a "Christian" church that was abundantly queer, nestled in the mountains, exploring what it means to be spiritual without a god. I can't think of a better place to oscillate between during our time in the south, my heart, mind, and body tethered between the rainy red mountains of Southern Virginia and spiritual agnostics in the high country. It's as though I can hear Pauli Murray whispering on the serpentine drive back, "Hope is a song in a weary throat. Give me a song of hope and a world where I can sing it."

The trees call out, dancing in their finest autumnal frocks, as I wind my way back toward Little Freya and my queer little family. We are creating a world where my heart could sing. A melody bursts from within as I write the song that would anchor the retreats I would lead in Boone: She Is. You Are. We Are. Holy. Worthwhile. Enough. Botanist and member of the Citizen Potawatomi Nation, Robin Wall Kimmerer, claims that the trees will teach us, if only we tune our ears to listen. Together, we sing in hopeful harmony of what this adventure may bring.

**Rain.**

Since it has been raining for ten days without pause, we decide to join a gym in nearby Marion. Soggy, we enter the fitness center, grateful for the childcare that accompanies gym membership and the major discount we'll receive for me being able to substitute as a certified fitness instructor. With Riah happy to be playing with new toys and children his age, Elizabeth and I settle into the chairs in the registration office. After several befuddled minutes of trying to figure out whether and how we were a family, the kind man with the thick Southern accent registers us. Group fitness, an elliptical trainer with views of the Jefferson National Forest, childcare, a warm pool, and hot, clean showers await us. Six days a week we'd visit the gym to escape the rains, give Riah age-appropriate social interaction, work out, and savor the sweet hot waters of a clean family shower.

Just as in Vermont, our volunteer work here in southern Virginia entails sweeping bathrooms, shoveling fire pits, directing campers, and handing out WiFi codes. Yes, in the middle of nowhere we have WiFi. This was an intentional decision by the Forestry service because there is no access to cell service at the campground. WiFi is present for safety in the case of an emergency. This is accompanied by one landline telephone at the host site, which is secured under a bucket to protect it from the rain. Each afternoon, upon completing our chores, we lift the bucket and call the gym to reserve our childcare time for the following morning.

Due to the constant downpours, we don't have many campers, so anytime someone arrives, we are a mixture of excitement and dread. Hurray…people! Or…do these hunters reeking of deer pee and swathed in confederate flags hate queer women? Are we safe? During one particularly thunderous torrent, a campervan pulls into the grounds. Celebrating a brief reprieve from the rains, I plop Riah in the jogging stroller, grab the welcome and WiFi information, and head off to greet the new visitors between stroller sprints.

Nancy and Jack had Hawai'i license plates and fling the door open with a robust, "Aloha!" After the typical welcome, I ask if they were from Hawai'i and what they are doing all the way in southern Virginia. Traversing the continent, their campervan had sprung a leak that only paused when parked, so they had stopped at the nearest campground they could find.

They were from Big Island. "No way," I shout, "We're doing a work exchange on the Big Island in two months. What side are you on?"

"East," Nancy replies.

"Where in the East?" I beg, expectantly.

"Puna."

And it turns out Nancy lives fewer than five miles from where our family is scheduled to live and work for winter. What a small, wondrous world.

While they repair their campervan, they offer many recommendations for things to do, people to meet, and what to expect. It is the grace of the world, aloha expanding nearly 6,000 from its source. Hope.

## Heteronormativity.

After several weeks of us regularly visiting the gym, the lady at the front desk asks Elizabeth if we are sisters. "No," she responds curtly as she ushers Riah to the childcare room. We're asked this all the time. The next day, the woman wants to know if we're cousins. Elizabeth's answer is the same. One day later, she just has to know. "So," pointing at Riah, "are you has mama, and she's his grandma?" she implores, pointing toward me. Hells no. While there are, indeed, women who are grandmothers at 34—and I don't say this to demean or belittle their experience—but there is absolutely no way in hell I look like I could be his grandmother. This is simply because I'm only one month older than my wife. How in the hell does this woman think I could be old enough to be my wife's mother?

This woman, and all the ladies she was gossiping with behind the counter, simply cannot fathom that we are both Riah's parents. Despite the fact that we signed up for the gym on the family plan, entered and exited the gym each day together, and used the family showers, it never even occurred to her that we might be married. That we could be a family. I'm all about proclaiming my queerness, shouting my love for my family from the rooftops, but I'm also acutely aware of the illusion of our safety. One in three women are sexually assaulted in their lifetimes. Two of us live in our camper. I've been threatened numerous times by straight men "offering" to rape me to "cure" my queerness. Given the ways I heard "that's gay," "faggot," and "pussy" roll of the dip lacquered tongues of the men in the weight room, sweat dripping from their red MAGA hats, I didn't have the emotional energy to stand atop the rowing machine and come out for the four thousandths time in my life. "I have announcement, Southern Virginia! This woman on the treadmill, the one who accompanies me and my child to the gym every single day, the one who showers with me in the family bathroom, the one wearing a matching wedding ring, well, she is my wife. We are queer. And the adorable child playing with model trains in the childcare facility is our son. We are a family! You may now return to your heteronormative exercises and enjoy watching Fox news."

This may not seem like that big of a deal. And, in isolation, it isn't. But questions and comments like these never happen in isolation. We're only four months into our full-time travel adventure and I cannot count the number of times we've had to explain, correct, or justify the queerness of our family. It's so fucking invalidating and exhausting.

Only days later, the rains pause long enough for campers to emerge, tents, hiking boots, and RVs at the ready. With every visitor who arrives, our gaydars are set to sound alarms if someone seems like a potential threat. As I chat with a man decked in camouflage and his wife clad in a light pink shirt with "Blessed" bedazzled across the chest in rhinestones, Elizabeth and Riah return from a hike. I scoop Riah into a hug as the bedazzled woman dripped, "And who is this little cutie pie?"
"This is my child, Riah."
Confused, she points at Elizabeth and places her hands on her hips, "And who might this be, then?"
"Oh, this is Elizabeth, my," and just as I am about to say "wife," the pink bedazzler interrupts me with the enthusiasm of a good, Southern, "Bless your heart," and says, "How sweeeeet! She's helping you watch your baby while your husbands are deployed in the military!"
Wait. What?!

There had been no mention of husbands. No talk of military. The thin silver bands around our left ring fingers matched each other. The child in my arms had clearly called me mama and Elizabeth mommy. And yet. Yet with all signs pointing toward the three of us being a family, this Blessed wife made the completely uninformed assumption that we were friends traveling together with my child while our imaginary "husbands" were deployed. You can't make this shit up. And I kid you not, we had a nearly identical conversation with another camping couple a few days later. Perhaps there was some group of traveling camper wives with deployed husbands that roamed Virginia's southlands that I simply wasn't aware of. More likely, heteronormativity still reigns supreme. *This* is not a world where Pauli Murray can sing her song of hope.

## Jokes.

When my father comes to visit again, pitching his tent in another grove of trees to soften the roar of his snores, he is utterly bewildered to learn of these stories, convinced that no one thought this way anymore. He'd never thought about it before. And this is precisely what straight privilege is: not having to think about it. It doesn't mean you can't or don't experience hardship. My dad, for example, has had a life filled with hardship, as he grew up in the projects with absent parents, didn't finish high school, and compensated for these losses with a thorough diet of addiction throughout much of his life. Straight people can, indeed, experience hardship. But they never experience hardship *because* of being straight. My family experiences hardship because of our queerness, but we still have white privilege because we never experience hardship due to our race. These seemed unfathomable concepts in confederate flag territory.

Adding to the quandary of the two ladies with a child camping together in the wilderness is the arrival of Riah's birth parents to celebrate his second birthday. As we prepared for their visit by figuring out how to rig a space heater in their tent, Riah's birth mom was coordinating a multi-state dog rescue from a kill shelter. The dog was in the Atlanta area, so my mom and brothers stepped in to help. As I talked with my middle brother, Carl, over the phone, I could tell something was off, but I couldn't put my finger on it. He just told me he was really happy that he'd lost 28 lbs. Brushing it off, I continued to relay messages between Riah's birth mom, my mom and brothers, the kill shelter, and another acquaintance making the drive to deliver the dog halfway.

Birth parents arrive with new dog, Papaya, in tow, and we celebrate Riah's second birthday with cupcakes and camping, vegan chili sizzling on the camp stove as we attempt to stay warm.

Because of this camp stove, we officially become the talk of the town in Sugar Grove, the tiny village closest to the campground, just after Riah's birth parents return to Michigan.

On a dark, cold evening just before Riah's bedtime, our Carbon Monoxide Detector rings for a few seconds while we finish eating dinner. We vacate the camper. Fortunately, it is just cold and not raining. Our camper's handbook indicates that you should call 911 anytime the detector rings. Since it only rang for a few seconds, and our camper was half built of canvas and screen, I thought this was a bit extreme, but still wanted to take precautions so as to not kill us all in our sleep. Using the landline phone hidden beneath the bucket, I call the local sheriff's station. I am informed that they're required to dispatch the fire department. I plead with them not to send a fire truck, or blaze sirens. Five minutes later an enormous red fire engine roars into the tiny campground, lights blazing, followed by four pick-up trucks. A total of fourteen volunteer firefighters show up; one manages to figure out how to work their Carbon Monoxide tester. Everything is fine, but the "two ladies with a toddler in a pop-up camper" will certainly the talk of the town for weeks to come. I hear they even sent word to our deployed husbands.

I return to Boone to lead Embodied Spirituality Retreats and preach for All Saints Day, inviting the community to join the subversive sisterhood of saints that formed our altera. Six paintings sell. Voices lift from among the ringing trees to join in our song of hope. My bin of icons substantially lighter, we complete our time in Southern Virginia by wrapping Riah in an owl costume for Halloween. Caring little for the candy, he is enamored by the construction trucks nearby and stands watching them, occasionally hooting at his grandparents who hold his sticky hands.

The day before we leave Virginia, we head to the gym as usual. Riah loves the water and relishes any opportunity to swim, even at just two years old. Splashing among the elders engaged in water aerobics, he offers up his first joke.

Holding a foam pool noodle in his tiny hands, he proclaims. "Noodle." Pretending to take a bite of the foam, he continues, "eat." Grinning slyly, he offers the punchline, "Joke."
"Noodle. Eat. Joke." Indeed, little one. We will count on his humorous antics the next morning to wake us up before the sun. Like a typical toddler,

he generally rises by 6am at the latest. This would give us ample time to pack up the camper, hitch, drive to the gym, workout, and shower in time to drive three hours to Elizabeth's mom's home on a North Carolina lake for a visit. "No need to set an alarm" we yawn the evening prior.

At 7:45am the next morning, we awake to hear Riah laughing on his side of the camper, "Noodle. Eat. Joke." We glance at the clock and realize that Riah has slept in the ONE TIME we counted on him not to. The next thirty minutes resemble the scene from Home Alone when the family slept in and left poor Kevin at home while rushing to the airport to fly to France. With our water tanks frozen solid, Elizabeth takes down the camper in record time, and we get to the gym disheveled, chilled, and in time for a shower. The lady at the front desk, and all the childcare workers, are still completely bamboozled by the makeup of our family. As we chug away from this strange place we've called home for a month, a notification on my phone pings the moment we had cell coverage. The book I'd worked on with one of my colleagues about microaggressions in ministry is officially published and available for purchase. My copy was in the mail to Atlanta, where we'd go after visiting Elizabeth's mom in the foothills.

**Microaggressions.**

"Our church is *colorblind*. Race just doesn't matter to us."
"You're the best *woman* preacher I've ever heard."
"It's fine if gay people want to get married, but I just worry about the *children*."

Statements like these are regular occurrences in the lives of persons of color, women, and LGBTQs. In our society, and in churches in particular, we like to think of ourselves as good, moral, thoughtful, open-minded people. We don't want to think that we—or our churches—are racist, sexist, or heterosexist. And yet marginalized persons continue to find themselves feeling invalidated, undercut, or unwelcome in subtle ways. These seeming subtleties add up over time in ways that assault the psyche, the body, and even the soul. These everyday subtleties that attack the souls of oppressed persons and groups are called microaggressions.

Microaggressions—subtle and often unintentional slights, insults, and indignities experienced by persons of varied minority statuses—occur on a regular basis in education, the workplace, and daily life. Drawing from my own experience of microaggressions that assaulted my soul so much that I left the Church altogether, I joined with a brilliant colleague, Rev. Dr. Cody Sanders to write *Microaggressions in Ministry: Confronting the Hidden Violence of Everyday Church.* Asserting that the context and language of religion can intensify the impact of microaggressions, our book provides examples and tools for grappling with microaggressions in preaching, religious education, worship, spirituality, pastoral care and counseling. Many are quick to quip at how much has changed, at how far we've come. Slavery was abolished. Women can now vote. As of this summer, LGBTQs can legally marry. "We're all treated equally," is the common refrain.

And yet my time in Virginia has been a blatant reminder that this is simply not true. Though society and facets of the church are eager to condemn blatant forms of racism, sexism, and heterosexism with the wave of a politically correct finger and a quick quote of Galatians 3, churches still manage to hurt, insult, and invalidate the souls of countless persons of color, women, and LGBTQs. We arrive in Atlanta, prepared for me to speak about this at my field's annual academic conference, at a local women's college, and at a feminist bookstore in my favorite part of town. Atlanta is the placed Elizabeth and I both grew up, and my mom, both brothers, and dad still live here. This is a homecoming of sorts, equal parts work and play. For me, a place of hope.

**Atlanta.**

Though Elizabeth's dad is retired in Florida, his entire career was in Atlanta, and as a realtor, he still manages properties in the area. This means we got to park the pop up in his garage and relish the luxuries of the place our family lovingly calls "The Treehouse." It's an apartment built over a two-car garage. Road weary from a five-hour drive towing a camper in Atlanta traffic with a not-so-eager toddler fussing in the backseat, we are too exhausted to figure out the best way to park the camper when we first arrive. So, we drive directly into the garage and decide we'll figure it out in the morning.

An inch by inch three-point turn morphs into a twenty-four-point turn as the squeaky Explorer wheels shuffle back and forth through the garage. We manage to U-turn it into the second space facing outward and ready to hit Atlanta's 7am-10am rush hour with gusto. This leaves us with a camper facing the wrong direction, and in desperate need of cleaning. It turns out that wheels make moving 3,000 pounds fairly easy, as we simply lift up the end and heft it around.

Vehicles in place, it is time to embrace the real reason we came to Atlanta. Not family. Not work. Not a few weeks of camping reprieve. One thing and one thing only. A steam shower. After over four months of borrowed showers, I will spend the better part of three weeks here oscillating between the steam shower and soaker tub. Both are ideal as we train for the Atlanta half marathon, welcoming the steam and jet streams on ageing bodies too achy to budge. Between lectures, training, and ample time spent cleansing my every pore in a bathroom bigger than our entire camper, we visit with my side of the family. Something continues to seem off about my brother Carl, but I relish the time he spends with his nephew building block towers and pillow forts as Riah giggles and proclaims, "joke" each time he plays a trick.

I give my lectures about microaggressions. Audiences are receptive, even engaging. The topic of faith arises at the feminist bookstore event when I shyly garner the courage to name my doubts aloud. Elizabeth is present and lingers with me as the crowd disperses and a few ardent feminists gather for deeper conversation. A radical nun pushes back on my tentative embrace of agnosticism when my wildly introverted wife speaks up. This is rare in a group of strangers, so what she has to say must be important. She speaks fervently of her Catholic upbringing, her so-called "Dorothy Day" years, and her recent conversion to atheism. She is resolute, yet gentle in her words. Concise and measuredly passionate. These are things I love about her. The nun is not happy about this. Committing what is ironically a religious microaggression, she informs Elizabeth that she must be going through a phase. She'd outgrow her doubts and embrace God again, the nun tells us both. Exchanging exhausted glances, we leave the feminist bookstore for veggie burgers. Apostates with fries, we savor grownup time away from our child and the nagging eye of a shaming nun.

The week prior to Thanksgiving, we drive to meet Elizabeth's side of the family at her brother's in Florida. Then we spend Thanksgiving contemplating the Day of Mourning as we run a half marathon. My mom graciously watches Riah while we run, and she simultaneously prepares a feast for our extended family. We all gather at my grandfather's muscadine vineyard, the log cabin and farm that punctuated so many pivotal points of my childhood. Famished and wobbly after running the half-marathon, I sit hungry by the potbelly stove when my brother Carl plops down beside me and tells me he plans to leave his job. Since I had found such freedom in following the beckoning into the unknown, I applaud his bravery, particularly after he assures me that he has diligently saved so that he can figure out what he wants to do next. Maybe this is what seemed off in him. His own beckoning to leave a job that was hurting him. I had no idea that his struggles with addiction had returned.

**Queer Holidays.**

It's no secret that the holidays are often a difficult time for queer people. Disproportionately estranged from family, we often must create our own family. While these chosen families can be tremendously life-giving, it's tough not to long for our families of origin during Christmas time. Many still in relationship with family are forced to retreat to the closet for fear of safety or exclusion this season.

Queer folk who have affirming families of origin still experience the twang of heteronormativity in holiday commercials, family events, and church services throughout December. There's a reason why many refer to it as "Blue Christmas," because, well, the holidays can leave us feeling pretty blue when our identities are invalidated, excluded, questioned, or marginalized.

In every nativity scene, we see images of a so-called "holy family" that likely doesn't look very much like the families most queer folk create: a straight, cisgender couple, and a baby. This family is lauded by the Church as the quintessential iteration of what family should look like. When our families don't look anything like this, it's easy to see how celebrating the birth of Jesus is fraught with emotional and spiritual hardship.

There is good news, though. We can subvert this narrative of traditional family by queering the story. So, I'd like to talk a bit about the revolutionary power of queering Mary and how she accompanies us, like those foreign "wise men" followed a bright star Westward. Abolitionist and Women's Rights Activist, Sojourner Truth, said it best at the 1851 Ohio Women's Convention. Once enslaved, Truth questioned the whitewashing done to women of color by white women working only for white women's right to vote by asking the famed question, "Ain't I a woman?" In that same speech,

68

she notes that male clergy claim that women "can't have as much rights as men 'cause Christ was a man."

This adage is familiar, not only to women, but also to LGBTQs who have been told that our iterations of family aren't real or true or right because they don't reflect the so-called holy family of Joseph, Mary, and Jesus. In an act of theological brilliance and subversion, Sojourner Truth poses this question to the male clergy gathered at the convention: "Where did your Christ come from? Where did your Christ come from? From God and a woman. Man had nothing to do with him!"

I'd contend that Truth's words queered traditional understandings of Mary. She was responsible for birthing Jesus, for ushering Emanuel into the world. Man had nothing to do with it. If we take this a step further, borrowing from feminist theology and boldly claiming that God is a She, then we queer the Christmas narrative even further. Mary and She Who Is (God) brought Jesus into the world. Jesus had two moms!

As I paint myriad cultural iterations of Mary, I think of Truth's subversive proclamation. I think of the difficulty of this season. I think of the hopeful potential of a Queer Mary that emboldens, empowers, and enlivens the queer community to be proud of who we are, to honor and celebrate the beauty of the families we create amidst outside threat. Mary knew a little something about the difficulty of creating a family amidst outside threat, didn't she? She wasn't married to Joseph, which was tremendously scandalous during her time. Scripture tells us she was a virgin, so that makes her pregnancy pretty complicated. She had to travel far while pregnant with Jesus. She gave birth in a manger because no one would welcome her family. And then the king wanted her child dead.

For those of us who have created queer families by bringing children into the world, we can relate to the hardship of Mary's pregnancy. It was two years before I had legal rights connecting me to my child because the government didn't dub my relationship with my wife legal; I was merely a legal stranger in our home. There are countless families who would never welcome us into their homes because they view our queer family as wrong, sinful, an abomination. Want to know about tough pregnancies? Ask a few queer families about the measures they had to take to bring a child into the world. And, yes, throughout the world there are "kings" (political leaders) who would rather have us dead than alive; their legislation reflects this.

So, I'd contend that Mary's very being, her family, and the entirety of Christmas is actually quite queer. I think of the borderlands where Our Lady of Guadalupe dwells in Mexico, embodying difference and diversity in one inspiring being. I think of La Negrita and how she chose to appear to least among us in Costa Rica. I think of the Virgin de la Caridad and her close association with Yoruban Oshun, saving all from watery chaos in Cuba, or the Virgin de la Regla's association with Yoruban Yemanya and her fierce love of all her children, including you and me. I think of Oya and her connection with Our Lady of Candelaria creating destruction in order to bring about winds of change and new life on the Canary Islands. I think of Mary—porous enough to cross and transgress and subvert and embrace all borders—birthing new life with She Who Is and ushering light into the world. And I am hopeful.

It's not that we must queer Mary's story or being. We simply must look close enough, peel back the layers of history, peak into the forgotten crevices of the canon, and trust our queer vision, for what we see is nothing less than a queer saint with a belly full of divinity embracing us in all our beautiful diversity. So, when you find yourself dwelling in the Christmas blues, remember that Mary's color in iconography is blue. Cling to her queer spirit and hold your head high, for divinity dwells within you, as well.

My hopeful queer family left the farm to embrace the blue, accompanied by Murray and Mary who embrace us still. We bid the beloved steam shower farewell, unsure of how we'd bathe as we prepared to spend the month traversing the southern border of the country to California. With timelines planned and stops scheduled, we navigated Atlanta traffic one last time, heading to the place where the sun is going, but has not yet been. Hope-filled places.

## Chapter 3: Creativity

# East-West Cross-Country Road Trip: Guadalupe and Gloria Anzaldúa

*"Voyager, there are no bridges, one builds them as one walks."*
*- Gloria Anzaldúa*

**Guadalupe.**

It is early morning on the Hill of Tepeyak on December 9, 1531 when a wondering peasant named Juan Diego first caught a glimpse of her presence. Diego sees a vision of a teenage girl surrounded by light; the young girl asks that a church be built on the hill in her honor. After hearing her speak and seeing the light emanating from her presence, Diego recognizes her as the Virgin Mary. He rushes to the Spanish archbishop who insists on a sign as proof of Diego's vision. The young girl instructs Diego to gather flowers from the top of the hill, even though it is past their growing season. Upon climbing to the top of the Hill of Tepeyak, Diego discovers Castilian roses—a beautiful flower otherwise unheard of in Mexico—which the glowing young woman arranges in his cloak. When Diego returns to the archbishop, he opens his cloak to reveal the miraculous flowers and they fall to floor; in their place was an image imprinted on the fabric of his cloak. It was the image of Our Lady of Guadalupe.

Guadalupe is one of Mexico's most popular religious and cultural images and her icon, now on display at the Basilica of Our Lady of Guadalupe, is one of the most visited Marian shrines in the entire world. On December 12, countless Christians—particularly Catholics—celebrate her feast day. Her feast day occurs within the four-week celebration of Advent, which is the period of waiting, expectancy, and gestation before the birth of Jesus at Christmas. The period when we traversed the southern border of our country.

Many feminists struggle with Mary and Our Lady of Guadalupe, insisting that they are often used to illustrate the submissive role of women in the church. Still others adhere to essentialist understandings of their stories, claiming liberation from some kind of inborn and innate feminine power. In these ways, some feminists highlight the story of Mary/Guadalupe as an example of the divine feminine nature of God, gestating in the womb and birthing the sacred into being. This is a powerful way of talking about divine incarnation, of God enfleshing Godself into earthly reality through the expanding womb of young Mary.

Yet, I was surprised when the time came for me to paint an icon in honor of Our Lady of Guadalupe. I'd intended to paint her for several years but struggled with how to find empowerment in her traditional iconography. Then I was commissioned to paint her as a gift for an amazing young woman. A father asked me to paint Guadalupe for his adult daughter, a midwife who works with babies born on the border between Mexico and the United States. He shared pictures of his daughter, told me about her inspiring work, and informed me that her favorite painting of Guadalupe subverted traditional iconography by placing her in a slinky blue dress covered with shimmering stars in the foreground; in the background it is clear that she stands among prostitutes. Inspired by this midwife and her work, my painting also subverts Guadalupe's traditional image. She wears the same blue dress, but continues to be surrounded by a halo of holiness as her heart proclaims:

> Birthing beauty into the borderlands,
> Her heart beat with compassion and dignity
> For all her beloved children.

These borderlands, and the beloved Guadalupe creatively birthed me. The magic of shrines, blossoming flowers, Guadalupe's solidarity with the poor, and the way she creatively manifests herself to both peasant and papal embolden creativity within me. Subverting, dismantling, reimagining, and the queering of the American dream takes creativity. Guadalupe's creativity. Her story lingers over our family as Little Freya hugs the southern border of the United States while we trek slowly Westward.

The first stop is Birmingham, Alabama to visit the Rodriguez side of my family, Guadalupe jostling in the enormous green bin of holiness in the camper's storage compartment. It's something my family doesn't speak of often, and when it's uttered it's often in hushed tones. I have yet to decipher the actual relationship of the extended relatives on my father's side. To be frank, it seems that my late mema—my father's mother—and her sister really got around. There are siblings and cousins with a host of last names, many stemming from this southern border, and there have been rumors that mema spent some time as a prostitute. Concrete answers are hard. Lo siento is easier. Silencio is the easiest.

Riah and my Rodriguez cousin's son are only one month apart in age and haven't yet met, so we have timed the first leg of our cross-country journey to pause in Birmingham at the borderland of family, wildly different worldviews, where welcome and hospitality are freely given. My cousin's primary concern as we cross the country is where we will decorate a Christmas tree and how Santa Claus will visit. Though I respond with a simple, "we don't do Santa Claus" her horror-struck face evokes the feeling we have any time we discuss this with other parents. It's not a very popular opinion, but we've told our little two-year-old the historical story of the Saint, and we don't really do the religious stuff of a baby god born in a manger, but we mostly don't want to lie to our kid and amp up his hopes for a bunch of consumerist plastic pouring out from under a tree that was supposedly delivered by a stranger breaking into our house.

"What about the magic? The wonder? The whimsy?" Believe me when I say, my child's life is overflowing with fucking magic. Fairy trails through overgrown forests, the sweet ballad of loons, frolicking through fall foliage, and the countless dazzling lights that fill our night sky across the country are natural magic, magic that fills his young eyes with the wonder a commodified myth simply cannot. I get it. I mean, I like Christmas décor, nostalgia, and the coziness of the season, but I'm not too worried about it as we cross the country. As we will soon find out, every campground is covered in decorations and Riah will sit beneath the dazzling light of more trimmed trees than we cared to count.

This encounter with extended family is a reminder that our queerness extends far beyond our sexuality in our family. We're a little weird, and this is difficult to grasp for some folks. And that's fine with me. We haven't completely rejected everything from mainstream society, but we dwell so firmly at the border that Our Lady of Guadalupe's identity resonates more and more deeply as we follow the sun West. Creatively queering and creatively queer.

73

**Remembering.**

From Birmingham we chug toward New Orleans. Swathed in Spanish moss, we spy the first of the holiday décor that will become the staple of our cross-country amble: an enormous alligator Santa. We sway to jazz along the river, eat beignets and pralines, and begin listening to the children's global music CD on repeat, as it soothes Riah on the long drives. As "King of the Bongo" croons through the speakers on our way past the levees, I receive a message that takes my breath away. It is from one of my former congregants, a trans man who facilitated the Transgender Support Group, a pivotal new member in the church until his soul was also assaulted by microaggressions from within the community. Another former congregant and member of the Transgender Support Group had just been found dead by suicide.

Her name was Emily. As a pastor, I was always happy to have someone new visit the congregation. So, I was particularly thrilled when Emily scheduled a meeting with me after visiting worship for the first time. During our meeting, Emily shared that she identified as a transgender woman, that her family had essentially disowned her, and that the conservative evangelical church of her upbringing would no longer welcome her. Emily had researched both the church and its pastor—me—thoroughly and knew that we offered LGBTQ Spirituality Groups and Transgender Support Groups, so she had high hopes that we would be a place of welcome.

For over a year, Emily and I met together and exchanged lengthy emails of theological and political depth. Through it all, Emily continued to use male pronouns and the name assigned to her at birth. She had much to lose. She was a well-respected doctor who could not imagine transitioning or being outed as transgender in the medical community where she served. When she received a fellowship to a prestigious and progressive medical institution far away from the hospital where she worked, Emily was confident that it could become a place to transition fully.
She moved away just before my child was born.

Our long theological emails ended, and I assumed Emily had found a place where she could thrive, authentically and fully herself. After welcoming my child into the world, I received a gift of global children's lullabies and a beautiful note from Emily. I think of her each night when I sing to my child. After this, we remained connected only through social media. I never imagined how much Emily continued to struggle. This is one of the countless privileges of being cisgender: not having to think about the daily struggle of being trans in a transphobic world. As I listen to the CD she mailed to celebrate the birth of our child, I learn that she is dead.

The bold, brave, brilliant woman whom I falsely assumed was thriving was gone. As a queer activist, I often think that I'm aware. I know the facts and figures. Over half the country allows gender identity discrimination. Trans women of color experience higher rates of police brutality. Trans women experience higher rates of sexual violence, homelessness, and employment discrimination. 72% of victims of anti-LGBT homicide are transgender women and 67% are trans women of color.

The next year in my home state of North Carolina, politicians will spend millions of taxpayer dollars to pass and uphold a law that regulates where trans people can use the bathroom. As a pastor, I also know that trans people are disproportionately ostracized from their families of origin and faith communities, violently assaulted by bully pulpits throughout the world. All these facts and figures were a lived reality throughout Emily's life.

Even though I knew these facts and figures, this knowledge could do nothing to bring her back. I have experienced a number of congregants dying or attempting suicide. This was the first time when I washed in guilt, asking the oft-repeated question, "What could I have done differently?" How could I have loved more fully? Should I have stayed in better contact after Emily moved? How could I have been so clouded by my own privilege that I did not notice she was struggling?
I am angry at myself for my lack of awareness of what Emily must have been experiencing.
In a world where trans people are demeaned, excluded, exoticized, invalidated, legislated against, and killed—the courage it takes for trans people to live fully into who they are is worthy of respect and honor. I dare say it is a holy act.

For the lives of trans women have something important and needed to teach the church. Emily taught me what it means to remain faithful when the world and the church are unfaithful to you. She taught me what it means to be authentically and fully human. Emily taught me what it means to be brave. She embodied Lilith, Jarena Lee, Sophia, Freya Stark, Mary, and Pauli Murray in radical ways. May we all be bold enough to live fully into our humanity, embracing and loving all unabashedly.

**Unhitched.**

Park. Unhitch. Camp. Hitch. Drive. Repeat. This is the mantra about every three days. Already, we are feeling too rushed. At each stop, there is enough time to explore for about a day if we pack the evenings with research for where to go next. New Orleans gives way to San Antonio, where magical lights dazzle on the river walk and we eat some of the most amazing vegan food at a cute little restaurant overlooking the water. Each night, we stroll through our different campgrounds scoping out the kitschy holiday décor pouring out of campers; you'd be surprised at people's creativity and how many camper-themed holiday decorations there are.

Before driving to Austin to visit friends, we cut green construction paper into triangles to make our own little family tree on the camper door. Riah decorates it with stickers as we write virtues we hope to embody in the coming year on red circles and tape them to the paper limbs: courage, integrity, hope, creativity, rage, care, interconnectedness, resilience, and love welcome us each time we open the door. A crooked star crafted by two-year-old hands perches atop our makeshift tree as we truck toward Austin. A creatively queer Christmas tree.

We continue our trend of visiting public libraries across the country for children's story time, this time reading in Spanish and English. In Austin, we see beloved friends, eat far too many vegan donuts, and continue to wonder the same question everyone has been asking us, "What the hell are you going to do in West Texas?"

West Texas ends up being much more beautiful than we expected. Literal tumbleweeds sweep across the flat plains, the expansive sunsets envelop us, and Elizabeth discovers Balmorhea State Park. The largest spring-fed swimming pool in the world, this state park was built by the Civilian Conservation Corps in the 1930s. Created by Roosevelt to provide job opportunities amid the Depression, the corps built a 1.3-acre pool around San Solomon Springs. Known as Mescalero Springs to the Mescalero Apache, it served as an oasis for water in the dry desert. December isn't exactly prime time for swimming, but that doesn't stop Elizabeth and Riah from donning their suits and jumping off the diving boards. I stand in a hoodie snapping photos of their chilly antics. Upon drying, Riah burns off more energy chasing roadrunners, and each night we take turns putting Riah to bed while the other mom walks through the desert campground under a dazzling night sky, grateful for these borderlands.

## Mansplanations.

As we prepare to leave, we experience some car trouble. It's something I anticipated because of battery issues prior to leaving on our adventure. So, we were prepared with a jump box. We are well on our way to jumping off the car, ready to hook up the camper and hit the road when a man approaches with a newer, shinier jump box. There is nothing wrong or mansplainy about his approaching. He simply notes that he saw our hood up and wanted to know if we needed help. This is a nice thing to do.

The mansplaination begins when he repeatedly refers to us as "sweetie," and "honey," while incorrectly showing me how to jump off my own car (the car we were already properly jumping off). He proceeds to give us advice about how to purchase a better jump box. Hear me clearly: there is *nothing* wrong with offering to help a woman with car trouble. Also hear me clearly: there *is* something wrong with assuming that the woman knows nothing about cars.

The West Texas man did sincerely seem to have good intentions, but he illustrated "benevolent sexism," which is the sweet kind of sexism that assumes women are incapable of handling any kind of "manly" situation, such as fixing a car. A word to men: don't be like this. Listen. Don't assume that women are incapable of anything. For all this mansplainer knows, I'm a mechanic.

On the bright side, for the bad rap that West Texas gets, it sure is beautiful. We enjoyed stunning desert views, expansive sunsets, and wide starry nights. I'd go back with my jump box in hand, darling.

The next morning, we head to another spot. I'm standing in the windswept Texas campground, Elizabeth towing the pop-up camper, as Riah babbles in the car seat. All I want to do is check in. That's it. Yet my feet remained tethered to the dusty ground as yet another Mansplainy McMansplainer drones on and on about how to tow and park a camper. When he finally pauses, he gestures back toward our tiny rig and ensures me that my "husband can figure it out." It's a small slight, a tiny invalidation I receive and expect at each and every campground where my queer little family unhitches as we traverse the country. I could correct him, explaining that my *wife* is driving our truck and that neither of us have or want a husband. And sometimes I do. I could ignore him. And sometimes I do. I could go off on a rant about heteronormativity and how exhausting and invalidating it is for every single person I meet to assume that I'm married to a man, or that my wife is my sister, or that we know nothing about towing or mechanics or camping all over the damn country. But I'm tired, my road-weary body aching at the borderlands of a gender and sexuality that render my family incomprehensible at campgrounds throughout the United States. I considered building a bridge, kindly calling Mansplainy McMansplainer into conversation about welcome and queerness. And I have. But not today. On this windy day under the wide Texas sky, I think of Gloria Anzaldúa, nestled among sister subversives in our enormous green bin of artwork, and I creatively embrace the borderlands of my existence. Because of her, I can.

## Borderlands.

Gloria Anzaldúa was an American scholar who focused on the intersections among queer theory, feminist theory, and Chicana cultural theory. Born in the Rio Grande Valley of south Texas, Anzaldúa also creatively bridged the borders of personal and academic writing, weaving together theory with lived experience, English with Spanish, and inviting readers into a new world—one she creatively called Mundo Zurdo—that transcended these seeming binaries.

In her book, *Borderlands/La Frontera: The New Mestiza*, she offers her personal experience of the oppression of Chicana lesbians, while addressing heteronormativity, colonialism, and male dominance. Her notion of a new mestiza offers a "new higher consciousness" that dismantles dualistic and oppositional forms of gender and sexuality. She creatively introduces the term mestizaje, which is a state beyond binaries that challenges Western dualism. Confronting her sexuality at the Mexico-Texas border, and within a family that internalized racism and sexism, forced Anzaldúa to build bridges between seemingly oppositional cultures and worldviews. Because of these embodied borderlands, she developed theories for the marginalities that exist in the interstitial spaces along borders. These endeavors were both brilliant and incredibly creative.

Partnering with Cherríe Moraga to edit *This Bridge Called My Back: Writings by Radical Women of Color*, Anzaldúa names the ways in which she is often asked to choose between loyalty to women, to people of color, or to the queer community, even though they are all vital pieces of herself. In creating a new world—Mundo Zurdo—she lives into all these borders of difference, poetically claiming:

> *"1,950 mile-long wound*
> *dividing a pueblo, a culture*
> *running down the length of my body,*
> *staking fence rods in my flesh,*
> *splits me, splits me*
> *me raja me raja*
> *This is my home*
> *this thin edge of barb wire."*

Often speaking of her devotion to la Virgen de Guadalupe, Yoruban orishás Yemayá and Oshún, or Nahuatl/Toltec divinities, she lamented that many scholars ignored the spiritual side of her work, creating yet another border between what is academic and what is sacred. In fact, it was Anzaldúa that gave us the creative language of spiritual activism. Her bridges are the bond that hold together this chasm, because education without the soul is no education at all.

Though she identified as a chicana lesbian, Anzaldúa also claimed an intentionally queer identity and wrote specifically for queer communities of color. In *Una lucha de fronteras*/A Struggle of Borders, she claims:

> Because I, a *mestiza,*
> continually walk out of one culture
> and into another,
> because I am in all cultures at the same time,
> *alma entre dos mundos, tres, cuatro,*
> *me zumba la cabeza con lo contradictorio.*
> *estoy norteada por todas las voces que me hablan*
> *simultáneamente.*

"I am all the voices that speak to me simultaneously." So, she learned to bridge and code switch. Think of the code-switching necessary when shifting languages, when speaking in a heteronormative culture. Think of

79

the bridges she miraculously built amidst these differences, amidst the barbed wire that constantly threatened to tear her apart, to split her.

Do you ever feel your body or soul split in two? Does it ever seem as though you have to be one version of yourself in one space, and another version of yourself in another space? Are you constantly translating your identity in order to maintain relationships with a homophobic family member, unconsciously racist friend, or sexist workplace? When the barbed wires of this bordered existence threaten to split you wide, remember Anzaldúa's creative bridging. Stand firmly on the bridge of your existence. Stretch your arms open wide, embracing every piece of yourself. And join Anzaldúa in creating a new world of justice and beauty that honors every piece of our fractured souls.

Supported by the bridge she built, surrounded by the desert that formed her and what she called "her spirit animal, the jaguar," Anzaldúa's arms stretch wide enough to fill the breach. Under Yemayá's moon and Oshún's sun, embraced by Guadalupe's stars, her heart cries out to us:

> Bridging the barbed
> beauty of borderlands with
> split tongue, su corazón se
> raja. And mundo zurdo
> was created, a new
> mestiza crossing
> beyond binaries…

The next time you find yourself faced with a Mansplainy McMansplainer, your feet planted at the windswept borders of difference, remember Anzaldúa and creatively build a bridge. If you have the energy, that bridge may be between you and the one questioning your existence. If you don't, perhaps that bridge may be between your heart and your soul, confident of your worth. Either bridge is brave, bold, and needed. When you are split in two, Anzaldúa's heart remains, beating alongside you, inspiring and emboldening you to take another creative step.

**Christmas Borders.**

Anzaldúa's creativity accompanies us as our green bin of revolutionaries continues building bridges in Las Cruces, New Mexico. Ambling through the desert, we teach Riah that cacti is plural for cactus, and he delights in pointing out every single cactus and grouped cacti, warning us to avoid their "sharp prickles." We go to dinner in the Old Messila, which twinkles in holiday lights draped over a gazebo where a couple dances to Christmas music. It's quiet, and not many people are out. We hear footsteps and a hearty "ho ho ho," turning to see a man dressed as Santa Claus carrying a handful of candy canes. He walks toward Riah, now dancing along to the music and running in circles around the trimmed gazebo. Santa hands Riah a candy cane. He responds with a "tank too." Though we don't do "Santa Claus" with him, it's a magical little moment with the lights and the music, the stars and the kind (albeit slightly creepy) stranger.

A massive windstorm cuts our time in New Mexico short, as we fear the canvas on the pop up might rip off, so we head to Tucson for Christmas Eve. Since snow was in the forecast for the campground, we decide that a holiday splurge in a hotel is due. Ever the mastermind behind subverting internet algorithms for hotel deals, Elizabeth pays $38 for us to stay at a swanky spot with a heated pool, hot tub, classically beautiful Arizona décor, and a breathtaking view. I look up the regular rate and realize she saved us nearly $200. With a moment to breathe and catch up on the news, Guadalupe and Anzaldua's calls to creative justice at the borderlands stir in my heart that Christmas Eve.

This holiday season, in the midst of our ever-repeating mass shootings and debates about the welcoming of Syrian refugees, I have seen a meme, a pithy quote, a bumper sticker time and time again amidst my fellow liberals: "If only we had a seasonally appropriate story about Middle Eastern people seeking refuge being turned away by the heartless."
Similarly, many have posted pictures of nativity scenes with a tongue-in-cheek quip, "I'm so glad people are placing these lawn ornaments in their yards to indicate that they welcome refugees into their homes."

Myriad articles have been published encouraging Christians to remember our calling to welcome the refugee, and as an ordained clergywoman doubting her beliefs, I affirm these thoughts. I believe it is our responsibility, as Christians and particularly as feminist Christians, to welcome the marginalized, the oppressed, the refugee. I am also a strong believer in the separation of church and state, a distinctive imperative both to my Baptist tradition and to my home country of the United States. So, in many ways, it doesn't really matter politically that my faith tradition teaches me to welcome the refugee because my country is not a Christian nation, but it does matter that the primary symbol of my country—the Statue of Liberty—proclaims boldly and without apology: "Give me your tired, your poor, Your huddled masses yearning to breathe free, The wretched refuse of your teeming shore. Send these, the homeless, tempest-tossed to me, I lift my lamp beside the golden door!"

It seems that much of the essence of the faith tradition that ordained me and my country embolden me to welcome the outcast, the marginalized, the poor, the refugee. Even if they're from Syria. Especially if they're from Syria.

To me, this seems obvious, but for too many in our country, and within this faith tradition, it is taboo, absurd, antithetical to all that the country or the Christian should stand for. While I think there is more nuancing necessary than what is embossed in the bumper sticker, meme, or pithy quote, I also think the essence rings true. Did Mary, Joseph, and the newborn Jesus fit the exact definition one uses to describe refugees today? Probably not. Is the situation precisely the same? No. But I do think that there is something to be said about an unwed teenage mother finding refuge in an unlikely place in the face of wonder, misunderstanding, and chaos. I think there is something this unwed teenage mother, huddled with her infant in a dank and smelly manger (or so the story goes), can teach us about welcoming those who are different.

As that wildly unbelievable nativity story continues, we are also taught that "wise men" travel from "the East," following an intrepid star to greet this newborn and his unwed teenage mother. These men from "the East" were also foreigners, different from any person Mary and Joseph had likely ever met. They probably looked differently, spoke differently, and certainly believed differently than Mary and Joseph's friends, family, and community. And yet this young couple welcomed them, the strange foreigners at the door with odd gifts and unique beliefs and inconceivable claims of following the stars through foreign land. To me, both the harboring of the holy family—this unwed teenage mother, a bewildered father, and this newborn god—and the welcoming of the "wise men" are stories of what it means to look in the eyes of difference with an attitude of embrace and wonder rather than with an attitude of fear and exclusion. Mary, Joseph, Jesus, and the "wise men" teach us what it means to welcome and be welcomed.

As the moon rises over the desert mountains, I think of welcome, bridging, queerness, creativity, and the holidays. I think of Anzaldúa and Guadalupe and my family of origin as I continue to wonder what is going on with Carl. He texted that he'd resigned from his job, but something still seemed off.

We celebrate Christmas creatively under a full moon at Picacho State Park, hiking to the peak, Riah continuing his trend of pointing out cacti with a firm warning: "Sharp prickles. Careful." We take a family jumping photo and do yoga under the full moon. My mom mailed us Christmas gifts, so we march through the campground—occasionally bursting into Riah's rendition of Jingle Bells—with new headlamps strapped across our foreheads. We give Riah one gift: a toy car. We drink hot chocolate and crank up the propane heater in the camper. We are happy. It's one of the best Christmases I've ever had. No tree. No big gifts. A full moon, my wife, and my child camping in the desert.

When I call my mom, brothers, and dad to wish them a Merry Christmas, something seems off with everyone. In three separate conversations, mom, Josh, and dad all share how worried they are about Carl. He has stopped returning calls and texts. His fastidious appearance has shifted. Instead of being neatly pressed, freshly showered, and sporting snazzy socks, Carl has been showing up late with lint in his hair, his buttons askew, and pants rolled haphazardly. He weighs only 128 pounds and he clearly hasn't showered in a long time.

I'd only just seen him a month prior over Thanksgiving, and while he had looked quite trim compared to his former self, he seemed fairly happy, intent on resigning from his job, figuring some "stuff" out, and saving for the future. Now, based on everything they've told me from two separate holiday gatherings—one with mom and one with dad—all signs are pointing toward addiction. Ten years prior, this wouldn't have been out of the ordinary. Around that time, Carl flatlined from alcohol poisoning. One nurse told us that he might not make it. Another said, "Maybe this will fix him." I wanted to punch her in the throat. And I'm an avowed pacifist.

But the past ten years have been fairly solid for Carl. Though he didn't graduate high school, he quickly taught himself Search Engine Optimization and other online marketing tools that made him invaluable at his company. I try talking to him about it, but he avoids the conversation, asking instead if we are spoiling Riah for Christmas. I ask him specifically if he is using, and he promises he isn't doing any drugs. I decide to trust him.

**Shit.**

From Arizona we make our way into California. We camp by the beach near our friends in San Diego. While there, I receive a frantic call from my mom. As I watch the sun sink into the Pacific, she shares that she just knows something is wrong with Carl, but he refuses to talk about it. My mother pleaded with him to tell us what was going on, to share why he was behaving the way he was. After days of not responding to calls or texts, my mother drove to his apartment and banged on the door for hours. She could hear the television blaring, but he never answered. She called and texted and pounded on the door. She visited the leasing office, concerned that Carl may be dead. Because he wasn't a minor, they couldn't open the door. She waited in her car. Hours later, Carl left his apartment disheveled and completely out of it. Mom confronted him, wailing tears none of us had ever seen her wail. Not through divorce. Not through single parenting. Not through cancer. Not even through the alcohol poisoning. He would not allow her in his apartment and denied there was a problem. On the phone, I can sense her tears, and feel so far away. So unable to help. I tell her I'll try to talk with him about it.

I call him, but he says he doesn't want to talk about it and reiterates that he isn't doing drugs, but that he is starting to run out of money. "Didn't you say you saved $20,000 last month?" I ask him. "Yeah, you know it doesn't last that long," he responds. My queer little family is living off less than $15,000 for an entire year. He says he has to go. I write him a long email, pouring out my heart and begging him to let us in, to just tell us what was going. I try to assure him that we love him and that we'd love him no matter what, that I can listen without judgement, and that if he needs help, we can work together get whatever help he needs. He never responds.

We leave the beach and drive halfway to the bay area, setting up camp in Visalia, which is the gateway to Sequoia National Park. Forget the magic of Christmas lights and Santa. There is nothing more magical than hiking through the sequoias in the snow on New Year's Day. Seriously. It is utterly stunning and completely worth the snow chains we have to buy for our tires in order to drive up the mountains.

But it also throws us into a state of cognitive dissonance. Juxtaposed with these stunning monoliths, with the glistening snow and fresh air and ancient redwoods, is the fact that we are camping in the San Joaquin Valley. And I'm not talking about contrasting microclimates, though there was over three feet of snow in the redwoods and a mere bite of frost in our campground. Rather, the dissonance stirs from this stunning beauty—the national treasure that is the Sequoia National Park—and the complete cesspool that is the San Joaquin Valley. And it's a cesspool that we've created. In many ways, these are the borderlands of Guadalupe and Anzaldúa. These are the planting grounds of the so-called American dream.

Did you know that the San Joaquin Valley has the highest water contamination rate in California and one of the highest in the country? Did you also know that it's where the vast majority of your produce comes from? Primarily due to fertilizer run-off, the water is virtually undrinkable. Yes, the water that washes all over almost all the food you eat is contaminated. Everywhere you go smells like piss or cow poo. Flanking either side of the highway are farms overflowing with cattle crammed into the tiniest of stalls awaiting slaughter. When the cattle farms end, orange groves begin. And by orange groves I mean enormous factories with cheerful signs reading "Cuties" and "Halos." There are trees, for sure. And to be honest, they are beautiful. But the toxins sprayed over them from airplanes are not. And the factories bearing the "farm fresh" names of the produce that fills our holiday stockings chug smoke and toxins into the air.

We know the names. I assign them as research projects to my students: Driscoll, Cutie, Halo. The main producer of our strawberries plant, grow, and harvest amidst the piss, the stench, the toxins. My students debate the ethics of such companies in my classes. We rage and tweet and write about how poorly the workers are treated, how harmful the practices are for the environment. Particularly when we discuss *The Sexual Politics of Meat*, we rage against factory farming with its unjust treatment of workers, the environment, and animals, of undocumented farmers literally drowning in lagoons of cow shit, or being forced to slit thousands of pig's throats a day until their sanity is on the brink and the company partners with ICE to deport them. These are all things I talk about and teach about and write about…from afar.

And here we are, setting up camp on the contaminated soil, peeling our damn clementines, purchasing water so that we can drink and brush our

85

teeth. As I stood on my rickety soap box, I wanted to do what I do in class, and what many of my students are quick to do upon first learning about unjust food practices. I wanted to wag my finger—or raise my middle one—at the CEOs of Driscoll, Halo, Cutie, at all the corporate greed that leads to creating an entire valley where all who live smell the shit of injustice, where the virtues of farmers are so burdened by poverty and the threat of deportation that they can't do anything about it. Instead, however, I have to hop off my soapbox and tell myself the same thing I tell my students when they simply want to blame "the man" for the unjust food system that reigns supreme: we created this.

The CEOs need critiquing. We all need to change our consumer practices so that we don't support companies that treat workers, the environment, and animals so inhumanely. But we are also responsible for this. We—you and me—are all responsible for the stench that wafts through the San Joaquin Valley. We have created a system that forces animals into unlivable pens, factories where workers drown in vats of manure, soil so filled with toxins that it seeps into otherwise good water, thus making it harmful to people and animals who drink it. The farmers who grow the majority of the food Americans eat are unable to drink their own damn water because it is so contaminated. This is clearly a broken, wretched, unjust, sinful system. And we are all culpable. This is a world we have created. Because we want California raspberries in our North Carolina oatmeal. Because we want tropical fruit in winter climates. Because we think the only way to get enough protein is by consuming animal flesh. Because we don't see the manure lagoons or smell the stench of the factory farms or taste the toxicity of the water. Because we don't see it, we act like it doesn't exist. So, we eat our Halos and dice our strawberries. The lungs of workers—most often poor persons of color—grow sick from toxins. The earth weeps contaminated water. Animals are slaughtered every twelve seconds. Unlike Anzaldúa, it does not split us, or form a barbed wire across our backs, because we can pretend it doesn't exist. But it does exist; this American dream promised to so many has become a putrid nightmare.

**The Examen.**

Beautiful redwoods. Adorable orange groves. Sweet land of liberty. And the stench of injustice fills our bellies. Is my brother dying? Is the planet? How can I creatively build bridges through these borderlands of injustice and beauty? These questions put me in an existential funk as I participate in my

86

annual practice of the Examen. The Examen is a devotional practice originating with Benedictine monks who examine each day by asking how they were faithful and how they needed improvement. Basically, it's like recounting where you were kind or excelled and where you needed to show more kindness or work harder. On New Year's Day, I sit with my journal and examine the past year, while looking ahead with hope, resolutions, plans, goals, and dreams. I pen these words:

*"While there are true resolutions I hope for in 2016, I'd like to resolve to take a longer view and to embody Wendell Berry's poem, 'The Peace of the Wild Things,' particularly:*
*'do not tax their lives with the forethought of grief'*
*and*
*'I rest in the grace of the world, and I am free.'*
*I have devoted all my adult life to the study and ministry of the grace of God. Ultimately, this has left me unquenched. While I've clung to the edges of faith for quite some years, I think the time has come to rest in the grace of the world: a world filled with beauty and terror that dies and resurrects over and over. Perhaps if I rest in this grace—savor it, marvel, create—perhaps then I will no longer tax myself with the forethought of grief, worry, anxiety, or the constant fear that I am not enough.*

With faith filtering out of my body, we arrive in the place we called home for five years, the bay that first stole my heart: Berkeley. Though, as with every stop along this cross-country journey, there isn't time to explore, play, or catch up with friends and colleagues. In two days, we need to store our camper with former congregants, pry open the green plastic bin to hang a Holy Woman Icons exhibit, and replace our winter coats with swimsuits as we prepare for our trip to the Big Island of Hawai'i. We'll return to the bay in three months and can visit and explore then.

As we eat dinner on the bed of an airport hotel, Riah experimenting with wearing big kid undies for the first time, we take a moment to reflect on this epic journey across the country, and the borderlands we called home for a month. Immediately, we agree that such a trip simply needs more time. It took too much time to prepare for each leg of the journey. Unhitch. Pop Up. Camp. Hitch. Repeat. was a refrain that grew weary after twenty iterations. Riah now parroted our behavior hitching and unhitching at each campground. Waving his little arm in a circle, he'd shout, "Cut. Cut. About three feet. Close. Cut right. Almost," while pretending to guide a camper.

87

There was never a lack of wonder along the way: vistas, mountains, deserts, oceans, full moons, night stars, big trees. There was also never a lack of planning to do! While we most certainly do not intend to complain about this amazing cross-country adventure, we have learned a couple things that will aid us in our return across the country next summer. Namely, we'd like to take more time. A month seems like plenty of time to cross the country, see some key sights, visit with friends. It's not. At least it's not for us. Popping up and taking down the camper—with a toddler—means we simply need more time everywhere we go. And having a toddler means we need more time, too. Since we're both still working—teaching online for Elizabeth and freelance writing for me—the time we typically dedicate to work, relaxation, and exercise was usually consumed by driving, planning, setting up, or taking down. We drove when Riah napped, which took away important work time. This isn't a complaint as much as it is a lesson learned. There is always more planning to do when you're traveling every few days. And as someone prone to taking on too many projects, I learned that agreeing to multiple freelance writing gigs while finishing a book project might not be the best idea while traveling across the country. Lesson learned. I hope.

This trip is an item on many people's bucket lists. It has been my second time traversing the entire country while hauling something big. This time it was a camper. Last time it was a U-Haul. It remains a gift filled with creative wonder, the borderlands of welcome etching places in our hearts, the life and legend of Guadalupe and Anzaldúa our constant companions. And we are also completely exhausted. Towing a home and a toddler across the country is tiring. Planning the details of each stop was draining. Grateful. Fortunate. And also tired. At this point, if we could make it through the long flight with a wiggly two-year-old, sitting on the beach with a Mai Tai sounded just right.

With the barbed wire of queer difference tearing places in our creative hearts, my little family travels to a new landscape, to a place that will teach us different ways of bridging with creativity and with rage.

## Chapter 4: Rage

# Hawai'i:
# Dorothy Day and Pele

*'Eli 'eli kau mai*
*Let awe possess me.*

Her pupils are so dilated that I can't quite discern the color of her eyes. I detect the slightest sliver of icy blue surrounding the massive inky dots now staring back at me. Otherwise, I would have assumed her eyes were completely black.

"Who are you?" she asks, dazed.

"Angela," I respond, slightly shocked that she doesn't recall that I am arriving today—family in tow—after over a year of correspondence.

"Who?" she repeats. The strung-out man sprawled across the battered sofa on her lanai shifts. Or maybe he twitched. Was he even alive?

"Dr. Yarber. The professor and yoga instructor."

Nothing.

Perhaps the expression on her face changes, as though her memory was sparked and she recalled our numerous phone conversations, endless emails, plans and schedules from the past year. If she does remember or her face alters, I can't tell because I am lost in her enormous pupils.

"My wife and I are volunteering for three months. Teaching yoga? Working on the farm? Leading retreats? We're supposed to stay in the farmhouse," I say with a disturbing combination of confidence and hesitation.

"Oh! You came in the wrong driveway," she says with an alarming chuckle.

I glance behind our small, green vehicle, the Echo we've rented from a friend of a friend's "rebel artist" friend. I can distinguish absolutely no other path into the jungle that surrounds us. In fact, as we turned onto the "driveway" only minutes prior, branches scraped the hood and limbs grazed the sides of our tiny car as Riah pointed at the Jurassic-looking ferns and implored, "Dinosaurs, mama?"

"No dinosaurs, honey."

"Jungle?"

"Yes, we are certainly in the jungle." Elizabeth gave me a worried look. I took a deep breath and slowly drove forward. Apparently, what awaited was the largest set of dilated pupils I've ever encountered. Not dilated like she'd had a medical procedure. Dilated like she'd been doing drugs every day since 1973. White Puna hippies, I'd later discover, are kind of a thing here.

We found this place on the Big Island of Hawai'i—an organic farm and retreat center—through a caretaking gazette. They accepted WWOOFers, and upon researching their website, I reached out to see if our skills might match their needs in creative ways. Elizabeth had successfully arranged two campground hosting positions for a stunning summer in Vermont and an equally beautiful fall enveloped in Virginia's finest foliage. I was solely responsible for Hawai'i, and it was becoming clearer by the moment that I had monumentally blown it.

The plan, artfully crafted over a year of thoughtful correspondence, was for me to teach yoga classes, Elizabeth to work on the farm, and for both of us to lead a few retreats based on our areas of expertise as professors. We'd function a bit like scholars in residence, while also getting our hands dirty. It was a winter sabbatical dream. In exchange, we would stay in the "rustic" farmhouse with our toddler and enjoy the beauty the Big Island has to offer, surrounded by the mana and magic of Puna. "Mana" doesn't translate neatly into English, but it carries the connotation of magical, spiritual healing power, and it's what Puna is known for. It was a good plan. A plan a creative Type-A personality like myself loves: equal parts freedom and scheduling. At that time, I didn't also know that Puna is known for *haole* hippies and meth heads.

Knowing that sections of the island were quarantined because of dengue fever, I'd asked the proprietor extensive questions about mosquitoes before we arrived. She assured me that none of the WWOOFers complained of bites and that they kept everything meticulously trimmed to ward off the unwanted pests. The dinosaur ferns battling for the lead in Little Shop of Horrors attested otherwise.

Baffled, I follow the dilated pupils to the "farmhouse" that will be our home for the next three months. I don't look Elizabeth in the eyes as she unbuckles our toddler from the car seat, but instead focus on our child's gleeful chirps of dinosaurs and jungles.

We were expecting rustic. Before adopting a child, we did our fair share of backpacking in the woods and plan to resume such adventures once Riah is four or five years old. We don't need much. We didn't have running water while living in a pop-up camper in Vermont for three months; we adored our time there. Hiking, beauty, swimming, sunsets, wild berries and chanterelle mushrooms, simple time together as a family: that was precisely what we wanted. Rustic is not the word I would use to describe the farmhouse. Squalor comes to mind. So does shithole.

To be fair, it is as clean as a screened deck in Jurassic Park could be. Because that's what it is. A screened deck. This would be fine except that the screens have gaping holes. It is as though there were miniature welcome signs for mosquitoes. "Dengue Fever: Welcome Here!" On our tour of the farmhouse, we learn that the water is not potable. "You get used to it," the owner says. Maybe she was being coy. I can't tell because I am still distracted by her damn pupils. I knew that the shower and toilet were shared, so I ask her to show me where they are. She drones on and on about how lucky we are to have flushing toilets. "No one in Puna has flush toilets," she tells us as she points in the direction of an outhouse with a mud floor. The pit toilets we cleaned in Vermont were more sanitary. The capacity to flush does not a clean toilet make. The shower is a spigot dripping onto muddy ground, a swarm of mosquitoes hovering midair.

I look at Elizabeth swatting the bloodsuckers and notice two fresh bites on Riah. "I'm seeing quite a few mosquitoes. It looks like we've been bitten several times while inside the farmhouse during the past five minutes. I'm concerned about protecting my child from dengue fever while sleeping and bathing," I tell her delicately, yet directly.

"We've only had two cases of dengue within 1,000 feet of the farm," she informs me nonchalantly. This is new news. There have only been 63 cases on the entire island thus far, and two cropped up on the very farm where I'd brought my two-year-old. Dengue fever can be fatal for toddlers.
"They went to the hospital and they're fine now. No one complains about mosquitoes here," the dilated pupils declare. Almost comically (in retrospect, not in reality), Elizabeth smashes a mosquito onto her arm. I wonder if the blood smeared across her forearm is filled with dengue. Am I merely being paranoid, I wonder, enraged?

91

"Well, I have stuff to do," the proprietor intones, "make yourself comfortable and I'll talk with you later about yoga."

I sit down next to Elizabeth. Riah jumps to reach a wooden mask that hung from one of the posts affixed to a scraggly screen. Placing it carefully in his hands, I encourage a time of play, hoping the sheer terror on my face might go undetected.

"Shall we unpack the car?" I ask Elizabeth, hiding under a guise of Type-A fear.

"Or we could get in the car and drive away," she responds, resolute.

I let out a deep, guttural, everything-in-my-aching-belly sigh. Dear goddess, she was as freaked out as me. I wasn't being a princess diva. This place really is a shithole.

"Where the hell will we go?" I ask her quietly, concerned that both the dilated pupils would over hear or our child would learn of our unease.

"We'll figure it out. We always do," she says gently.

She was right. We always do.

We take out the iPad, preloaded with 1970s Sesame Street for emergencies. This is most certainly an emergency, and Big Bird is the best we could offer. Delighted at the treat of screen-time, our kiddo clutches the wooden mask and watches, unaware that his moms are having a minor meltdown. We can now have a conversation without unnecessarily leaking our fear onto an unsuspecting toddler. The last thing we want to do is scare our child after eleven hours of flying and a six-hour time change. I suppose that is the second to last thing we want to do. The last thing we want to do is give our child dengue fever.

I decide to walk the grounds. Just in case. You know, maybe walking around will give me another perspective on the place. Put me at ease. Make me forget the freakishly dilated pupils and how they are probably cooking up a big pot-o-Meth just around the corner. Within ten steps a giant rat runs in front of me. Intent on not being a total princess, I keep walking. When I pass another rat, my mind is made up. You can't get me in the tiny car fast enough. Now, to make it out of this jungle without destroying the rented vehicle.

I feel like such a failure. How could someone so good at planning, so organized, take such a misstep? After a year of conversations, how did I miss that this place and its owner are such a complete disaster? Am I just tired after six months of travel with a toddler? Have I become a princess who can't rough it anymore? Did I just endanger my child's life? We've spent a good sum of money flying to this island, intent on fulfilling our commitments to living differently and creatively and simply. What will come of our time in this beautiful place? It is as though the innate beauty of the island was mocking my misfortune. Where did I go so wrong?

We pile into the car and leave after determining that it would be best for me to email the dilated pupils later that day. Who knew what she would do in person, not to mention the twitching body sprawled across her lanai? We pull the car over at a public beach to make plans. Riah is entertained with palm fronds. We decide to stay at a hotel in Hilo for a couple nights to reevaluate the situation and make plans. On the drive there, we stop for $1 vegan tacos in Pahoa. Sensing distress, the taco stand owner asks me what is wrong. I truncate our story into two minutes and she responds quickly, "That happens a lot in Puna." Good to know. At least we aren't alone, I suppose.

Upon checking into a mosquito-free hotel with no dilated pupils in sight, I sign onto WiFi and email every single person I know in the entire state of Hawai'i. All four of them. Fortunately, I am also scheduled to be an interim preacher at the Unitarian church on Oahu, and my primary contact there hears my distress clearly: dengue, toddler, drugs, help! He emailed every Unitarian on the Big Island and within hours, the spirit of aloha Hawai'i is known for was manifest in my overflowing in-box.

"Sometimes Pele invites chaos because she has something more beautiful in store for you," a Buddhist friend on the island tells me. I suppose I knew this in my head and felt uneasily confident that it would become true, but in those moments in the farmhouse my primary concern had been protecting my child, which is something I couldn't trust Pele to do for me in the middle of the dengue-infested jungle. We share a brief and breathtaking night with this Buddhist friend in Ka'u, where she claimed, "What we lack in amenities we make up for in magic." As if on cue, peacock strutted by as she finished the sentence. Since one of the amenities she lacked was toilets, we spent the evening squatting in the darkness under the most dazzling canopy of stars I'd ever seen in my entire life. Wayfarers, indeed.

**Pele's Plans.**

Pele is a goddess of destruction, but her destruction is an imperative part of the creation process. The Hawai'ian Volcano Goddess who governs fire, lightening, volcanoes, and the flow of lava, Pele, destroys in order to create new life and new beginnings. According to legend, she lives in the Halema'uma'u crater of Kilauea on Hawai'i Island. There are several legends associated with Pele in Hawaiian mythology, but the one most repeated involves a fiery woman living on an island in the middle of the ocean. Whenever she became enraged, her lava devoured the land. Pele needed to find a home that could withstand her fiery passion and rage. No matter where she searched, lava raged and the oceans boiled. As she destroyed with fire, she also created. Each lava flow birthed new land where sprouts would push through the black rock. Sprouts became trees. Trees produced fruit. And all 'āina was nourished. Yet this nature could not flourish when she was present.

Pele realized that there was no perfect island that could withhold her passion, destruction, and creativity. So, she created her own home by striking her 'ō'ō against the ground to form a crater, bubbling with lava. She climbed inside, knowing that this was home. In this new home, she could rage, destroy, and create unencumbered. Even today, an average of five acres of new land is created along Hawai'i Island's shoreline each month because of lava flow. As Pele destroys, she also creates. New land is born from rage and creativity.

Her powerful legends remind us of the power of balance between destruction and creation. They also teach us to be mindful of the things in our own lives that must be destroyed for new life and new beginnings to sprout forth. The destruction is not always easy, and often involves the need for anger, rage, passion, and righteous indignation. When these attributes are so often viewed as negative for women, Pele's fiery spirit reminds us that we sometimes need to stoke our rage and passion in order to destroy what is no longer good, true, or just. Out of this destruction, newness may begin.

With arms reaching up to fire and lightning, her volcanic body pours over the earth, and yet the smallest of sprouts push through to create new life. Attempting to be mindful of what needed destruction in my life, I am eager to learn as much as I can about Hawai'i's culture and myths, intent on allowing Pele to destroy even the things I love most: my carefully crafted plans.

It turns out there is a cool couple—Unitarian astrophysicists—who have a small studio apartment they rent out, and their renter has just broken the lease. They also need a lot of work done in their yard. In exchange for ten hours of weeding a week, they invite us to stay in their little studio. Hilo Bay beckons us from the view on the driveway as we pull an infinite number of ferns and cane grass from the ground.

We quickly begin filling our days by exploring this stunning island as rainbows, beaches, sea turtles, mangos, rambutan, lilikoi, and banyan trees become our daily existence, and our pile of pulled weeds grows taller and taller. As we explore, we also research as much as we can about Hawaiian history, culture, and myth, while simultaneously endeavoring to listen deeply to our new *kānaka maoli* friends.

**Culture and Cosmos.**

We have come to Hawai'i as *haolē* (White people), not entirely unlike the colonizers who conquered and stole Hawai'ian land with the arrival of Captain Cook in 1778. Because of this, it's imperative that we critically examine our role in Hawai'i, particularly as so many *kānaka maoli* (Native Hawaiians) are rendered homeless by the ongoing occupation of their land. Even though *kānaka maoli* make up only 10% of the state's population, they comprise about one-third of the homeless population. Why?

Well, Queen Lili'uokalani was illegally overthrown by the American government in 1893, forcibly signing away her monarchy with the threat of killing key *kānaka* via hanging, and the presence of Christian missionaries and colonizers slowly dwindled the otherwise vibrant *kānaka maoli* population. In 1898, Hawai'i was annexed by the US and officially became a state in 1959. Now, the US military controls over 25% of the land mass on Oahu alone, and owns over 230,000 acres of Hawaiian land. Currently, tourists outnumber residents 6 to 1 and Native Hawaiians 30 to 1.

What does it mean to be a queer intersectionally ecofeminist family on occupied and colonized land? We are still trying to answer this question, confident that there are not easy answers. As we seek to become accomplices in the movements for Hawai'ian Sovereignty and Aloha 'Āina, we focus on listening and researching, drawing upon the rich work of feminist and queer scholar-activists like Haunani-Kay Trask, Leilani

Holmes, Kaumakaiwa Kanaka'ole, Lilikalā K. Kame'eleihiwa, Mahealani Joy, and Lisa Kahaleole Hall.

These Hawai'ian scholar-activists remind us of colonization's present reality in the exoticization of Hawaiian bodies (hello, grass skirt and coconut bra), its erasure of a Hawaiian presence even within many indigenous movements, and its commodification of Hawaiian culture. Even though original colonizers banned Hawaiian language, traditional clothing, and the worship of Hawaiian gods and goddesses, the aloha spirit is now commodified and packaged to sell to tourists. The moment it became profitable, Christian missionaries baptized "aloha" as a mode for conversion; soon after, kitschy hula costumes and plastic flower leis were imported without even a nod to the history of the hula, oli, and spiritual presence embedded in the land and cosmology of Hawaiian mythology.

Most people outside of Hawai'i only know of this commercialized version of aloha. But what about other powerful virtues, such as *pono* (righteousness), *maná* (spiritual power), *'ohana* (family), or *māhū* (third gender)? As a queer scholar, I learned about *māhū* before coming to Hawai'i, primarily from the resilient work of transgender black Hawaiian activist, Janet Mock. While it is incorrect to claim that *māhū* is synonymous with the term transgender, Mock and *kānaka maoli* activist, Kaumakaiwa Kanaka'ole, speak of *māhū* as the expression of the third self, outside of traditional gender binaries. Lisa Kahaleole Hall proposes that the erasure of *māhū* and the "deliberate destruction of non-heteronormative and monogamous social relationships, the indigenous languages that could conceptualize these relationships, and the cultural practices that celebrated them has been inextricable from the simultaneous colonial expropriation of land and natural resources (Hall, "Strategies of Erasure, 278)." We refuse to be a part of this strategic erasure. As a *haolē* queer feminist now volunteering in Hawai'i, it is incumbent on me to share these histories and to support the voices of *kānaka maoli* who have been telling these stories for generations. It is incumbent on me to share in Pele's rage at the way *kānaka maoli* and the *'āina* have been treated, predominantly at the hands of people who look like me. White people. Haole.

Lilith and Jarena Lee's courage leads us to the integrity of our callings with Sophia and Freya Stark. This integrity ushers in space for hope, emboldened by Pauli Murray and Mary. And hope is manifest in the creativity of Guadalupe and Gloria Anzaldúa. Believe it or not, rage is a natural expression of these virtues. Pele and this stunning island of Hawai'i are beautiful expressions of such rage, righteous indignation at injustice, colonization, and the commodification of a strategically erased culture.

If we remember that aloha doesn't simply mean "hello," but implies "compassionately facing the life-presence in all '*āina*," perhaps Hawai'i—and all '*āina*—can be a more just and beautiful place, indeed. This aloha, this newfound knowledge, and the spirit of Pele accompanies us as we make friends with other queer mamas on the island, as we welcome my dad and Elizabeth's parents again for visits. To black, white, and green sand beaches, encounters with monk seals and sea horse, on the rim of an active volcano and under the shade of a Monkeypod tree, Pele and the Hawaiian pantheon are here. They accompany us as we begin to seriously consider whether we could call this breathtaking place home.

**Calling Us Home.**

With the dilated pupils seeming like a distant memory, we decide it would be fun to look online at real estate. Part of traveling for a year was to discern a place to buy property so we can create an intersectionally ecofeminist retreat center. "Let's see how ridiculously expensive it is," Elizabeth laughs. Cue jaws dropping to the floor, tongues rolling out of mouths, and eyes bulging from our foreheads. Apparently, land and building on the Big Island costs less than anything we looked at in the southeast.

With its mana and magic, dengue and dinosaur-ferns. We begin to search in earnest, still grappling with what it means for us to be on an occupied island. I read *Haolēs in Hawai'i* and commit that I would only be the first type of haolē. The story goes that a professor was asked whether haolē was a racist term for white people. Knowing that reverse racism is a myth promoted by white supremacy, the professor responded by saying, "Look, there are three types of haolēs, and you can be any of the three. You can be a haolē. You can be a dumb haolē. Or you can be a dumb, fuckin' haolē." Whether we move here or not, one thing is for certain, I don't want to be a dumb fuckin' haolē.

Many people who relocate to the island speak of how they didn't choose Hawai'i, but Hawai'i chose them. While I don't know if I'd use this language, I will say that the multiculturalism, the rich history, the natural

97

beauty, the simplicity of off-grid sustainable living, the access to delicious vegan food, the ability to spend the bulk of your time outside, and opportunities to grow your own food called us to make this place home. Plus, we want to raise our child in a place where the majority of the children aren't white kids who only speak English. We don't want to exploit or commodify the diversity of the island—known as the most racially and ethnically diverse county in the country—but to relish, savor, and learn from it with gratitude. To raise our child to be an accomplice in anti-racism work. Looking back, I cannot help but question whether we were actually opportunity hoarding.

With these new realities weighing on my heart and Pele continuing to destroy my plans, I leave my queer little family on the Big Island while I fly to Oahu to serve as an interim preacher at a Unitarian Universalist church in Honolulu. It is yet another opportunity for me to trouble the waters of spiritual non-theism. After preaching and leading workshops, I climb Diamond Head, run on white sand beaches, and savor sumptuous mornings of sleeping past 6am. This savoring is salted by more conversations with my family in Atlanta as Carl's problems intensify. Now, accompanying his weight loss, unpredictability, disheveled appearance, and lack of responsiveness, he sometimes shows up with mysterious wounds on his face, as though he has fallen or been in a fight. All of us have begged him to tell us what is going on, assuring him of our love and care for him, promising to offer help if only he'd open up enough to tell us what is going on. I call him from Waikiki and he skirts my questions and offers, steering our conversations toward jokes, sarcasm, and questions about his beloved nephew. He is pretty stoked that Riah likes to wear his big kid undies backward. Both Carl and Josh often wore their undies backward when they were little because they liked to be able to see the cartoon picture that was printed on the butt. Our conversation never finds depth or honesty. I hang up after saying, "I love you," and return to the Big Island.

While I was away, Elizabeth and Riah finalized the details on finding an acre our family could call home once we finished our traveling adventure. Four blocks from the most stunning lava cliffs I've ever seen, an ideal spot for whale watching, without a mosquito in sight, we have found the place we wanted to call home. You can hear the ocean crash into the cliffs from beside the mango tree perched at the corner of our lot. As we begin plans to build and create, sustain and empower, our retreat at the forefront of our imaginations and hopes and dreams, I cannot help but think of the jungle's wild welcome and wonder if Pele was testing us.

Maybe Pele did have something more beautiful in store for our little family. With this generous, restorative offer of beauty, she has given us an opportunity to extend this same grace to others. So, we create, sustain, and empower a little retreat center on the Big Island in the middle of the startlingly blue Pacific. Off-grid and organic, much like the original place we visited. We'll do our best to keep the ferns trimmed and the welcome warm because, on Big Island, there's enough mana for us all.

As we seek out wisdom, builders, architects, and dream of what our family's future might hold, I sketch the biggest house we can afford on graph paper. A tiny off-grid home, complete with solar power and water catchment is our plan. Since it will be just under 500 square feet, I decide to look up how the television show Tiny House Nation does its casting. Lo and behold, anyone can apply. So, I decide to carefully craft an application and send it in. What do I have to lose? They have never had queer folks on the show, and they have never filmed in Hawai'i, so the uniqueness of our family might set us apart. I send in our application just before Holy Week, and though I no longer celebrate this Christian season, it falls on the twelfth anniversary of my ordination this year, so it gives me pause to reflect on where I've come from and where I am going vocationally.

**Ordination.**

Around the time we arrived in Vermont in early July 2015, I read Wendell Berry's poem, "The Peace of the Wild Things," with intention. It was fitting that I did so at the beginning of this wild adventure as the final line has become my travel mantra of sorts: *I rest in the grace of the world, and am free.*

The twelfth anniversary of my ordination, which always falls on the Spring Equinox, also begins Holy Week this year, so it seems like the perfect time to marinate on this seeming paradox: the grace of the world. You see, as a clergywoman ordained in the Christian tradition, most of my adult life has been dedicated to preaching and teaching about the grace of *God*…at least that is what I'm supposed to do. From the outset of my clerical work, I've never quite grasped the theological concept of grace. As a professional dancer, I had a handle on grace. It's what dancers do. Or at least what we're supposed to do. The grace of the world is something that was taken away by a conservative church that told me, in the words of James, that one cannot love God and the world. This didn't coincide with my overall worldview—the world is filled with beauty and grace, resurrection and redemption that existed long before Christianity baptized the terms and dubbed them theological—but for a brief period of time I decided that I simply must hate the world. Bless the soul of an undergraduate professor of religion who taught me that people of faith can, indeed, love the world, and that our duty is to love it so deeply and madly that we do everything in our power to make it more just and beautiful.

Along the way, however, I've opted to let go of this theological notion of grace altogether, namely because I've let go of the notion of a theos, the Greek word for God that begins "*theo*logy," or the study of the nature of God. Not in an antagonistic manner, nor with a tremendous amount of certainty, hence my dancing around the word "atheism." Always dancing. It's not so much that I'm a pantheist or even a panentheist because one can't really be either of those things without the theist part. Not god in the world. Not that the world is god. Rather, the world itself is sacred. We are sacred. Sacredness isn't confined by a god. Nor is holiness. Or resurrection. Or redemption. I've worried about how this reflects, or doesn't reflect, the nature of my ordination. But I still feel the call to preach and work and maybe even pray on behalf of communities otherwise excluded within orthodox traditions. It's just that my language for describing it has shifted. Elizabeth tells me I'm a strategic theist in the same way many feminists are strategic essentialists, knowing full well that using the word "woman" actually needs a lengthy footnote in the same way that any time I employ the word "god" would need a footnote much longer than this book. I only use the g-word strategically, politically, on behalf of marginalized communities who have been told God abhors and damns who they are. A strategic theist.

Because, when a queer person has had a parent beat the shit out of them, disown them, and left them homeless all because of a wretched exclusive theology, and that queer person comes to me and asks me to pray on their behalf, I'm not going to respond, "Well, actually, I believe God is a sociohistorical construct that may not exist." That would make me an asshole. Instead, I take their hands in mine, bow my head, and invoke a God who artfully created them with intention and abiding love, who weeps alongside them and who grieves a parent who cannot embrace the fullness of their humanity. I cannot abandon that part of my call, even if I've abandoned God. I will strategically call on God on behalf of these marginalized kindred, even if I do not believe there is truly a God to call upon. I will pray and preach on behalf of those excluded and damned, my ordination held with an open hand. If the God/dess I constructed over the course of my ministry actually is real, I have a feeling She'll be ok with my honest doubts.

All those meandering caveats lead me to say this. The grace of this world has never ceased to astound me. I recall reading a commentary by Barbara Brown Taylor in preparation for the first time I was to preach on an Easter Sunday. She admonished preachers to be certain of their theology of resurrection before preaching a sermon that equates resurrection with the stirring of spring out of the dormant death of cold winter. It's one of the few times that I've disagreed with Taylor. Otherwise, I think she's pretty damn fabulous. For me, however, the fact that the cold dark earth rebirths plants and flowers and leaves and new life every year is precisely what resurrection is. It's the grace of the world. Every. Single. Year.

It's no accident that I was ordained on the Spring Equinox. As we prepare to leave the Big Island of Hawai'i, our lives now turned inside out in the most beautiful way with the knowledge that we will return to call this place home, I am once again resting in the grace of the world. The grace that explodes in volcanic ash and then resurrects as green sprouts push through the black rubble. The sprouts turn to trees. Fruit grows. Our bodies are nourished. We are free. As Holy Week begins, devoid of any worshipping community or church services (by choice and with gratitude), I revel in this beautiful grace. The week begins so holy. But then it turns, once again, to rage.

Because my home state of North Carolina tromps into Holy Week with an early crucifixion, stringing the least among us—namely our transgender friends and neighbors—onto a cross of the legislature's own devising and reminding me that the world also has the capacity for great violence and harm. Yes, the lava that flows destroys and new life is eventually reborn, but there's no malice in the volcano's intentions. What North Carolina's legislators have done in HB2 is nothing short of malice and fear. Crucifixions aren't just a thing of the past. Neither is discrimination. Many people of faith hold this view. Many people without faith do, as well. I hold all this from a distance, on an island in the middle of the Pacific where the earth's core bubbles to the surface with fire, redemption, and resurrection, so far away from the place I called home for five years. It is for these reasons that I want to keep my ordination, though my beliefs—or lack thereof—have shifted. Because the least among us need to know that there are ordained clergy who will not tolerate such injustice. I may even opt to strategically employ the word "God" and claim that God weeps and rages at the sight of such injustice, as well. Can't you hear Her?

After these twelve years, I hold my ordination with an open hand. I was worried it could be revoked when I came out as gay a decade ago. And it didn't happen. Sometimes I worry now that this worldly grace may come at a cost, the cost of a theological grace being withheld to the extent that I may not be able to practice my ordination. I don't think that will happen. I hope it won't. In the meantime, I will rest in the grace of this stunning world, offering freedom to whomever I may encounter. Life springs eternal. Daffodils push through snow. Green sprouts burst out of lava. There's enough resurrection for us all.

**Simplicity.**

Pele's rage guides me in a surprising direction as I draft endless iterations of a tiny off-grid home on graph paper. Out of her destruction, new creations are formed. And I feel more and more confident that anything new my family is called to create must be simple. This simplicity led me to the woman who embodied it most: Dorothy Day.

Radical Revolutionary. One with the workers. Daily works of mercy. One who challenged the status quo. She never wanted to be called a saint, though the Claretian Missionaries proposed that she be canonized in 1983. The Catholic Church calls her a "Servant of God." I call her a Holy Woman Icon.

Born on November 8, 1897, Dorothy Day's radical spirit, her development of the Catholic Worker Movement, and her solidarity with the poor have taught countless women what it means to be a revolutionary. This American anarchist and activist converted to Catholicism as an adult after living what many describe as a bohemian lifestyle. She advocated the Catholic economic theory of distributism, daily works of mercy, pacifism, and solidarity with the poor. Rage began both her career and her conversion.

She started her career as a journalist, writing for Socialist publications, such as *The Liberator, The Masses,* and *The Call.* She was rumored to say to other Socialists that she was "a pacifist even in the class war." Her radical stances on workers' rights and class warfare combined with progressive Catholic social teaching when she joined with Peter Maurin to establish the Catholic Worker Movement. The Catholic Worker Movement began with the publication of the *Catholic Worker* in 1933, exuding progressive Catholic social teachings in the midst of the Great Depression and a pacifist position in the midst of war. The publication expanded to include houses of hospitality in the slums of New York City. These hospitality houses flourish all over the world today as intentional communities—urban and farm— where people live together communally, providing direct aid for the poor and homeless, while also advocating for nonviolent action on their behalf.

Throughout her life Day was arrested numerous times for civil disobedience, always standing in solidarity with poor workers, sometimes participating in hunger strikes until justice was given. By the 1960s she was called the first hippie and a few years before her death in 1980 she joined Cesar Chavez in California to support his work to provide justice for farm laborers. She was arrested with the other protestors, and at the age of 75 spent ten days in jail. No stranger to rage, her righteous indignation fueled her daily works for justice as she committed to creating a more just world for all.

As it did in life, Dorothy Day's heart takes center stage on the canvas. She is surrounded by nary an embellishment, living and loving simply and truly, her heart cries out to us:

> *Radically authentic, she*
> *Poured out her heart on*
> *Behalf of the least of these—*
> *The poor became her family, her faith,*
> *Her home*

Radical Revolutionary. One with the workers. Daily works of mercy. One who challenged the status quo. These are all attributes I strive toward as a queer feminist. So, it's no surprise that we gave Riah the middle name Day when he was born. His namesake joins Pele in guiding us toward radical simplicity and sustainable living. For it is through their rage, that Pele and

Day create what the world needs. And it is through our rage that we endeavor to do the same.

Where are you raging, subversive sister saint? What about your life and our world enrages you? In what ways has your rage been silenced, pushed inside in favor of "niceness," decorum, or politeness? Might Pele and Dorothy Day unleash this rage stirring within?

Pele's rage is a necessary and desired part of Hawaiian cosmology. Without her rage, so many imperative myths, legends, and lessons would be missing. She offers women an outlet for rage, affirming that righteous indignation is part of being fully human. Martin Luther King, Jr. called Hawai'i a manifestation of the beloved community, and myriad articles claim that "if you want to be less racist, move to Hawai'i." While it's true that diversity thrives here in the most racially and ethnically diverse place in the nation, if these claims aren't nuanced, they sometimes overlook the tremendous damage white people have perpetuated—and continue to perpetuate—on the Hawaiian islands and her people. This is something that should rightfully enrage us.

Lacking rage in favor of decorum is not polite, nice, or just. It is privileged. We need Pele's rage to move forward, radically imagining a better world. Dorothy Day embodies this rage, but expresses it differently. Both iterations of rage are important for emboldening radical imagination in us all. Day's rage stems from bearing witness to poverty, unjust economics, and war. Her rage led to living in solidarity with the poor, advocating distributism, protests, hunger strikes, and civil disobedience resulting in arrest and imprisonment. This rage fueled radical imagination, dreaming and creating a more just, beautiful, and peaceful world for all.

As Pele destroys, Day's rage guides us in creating new life with simplicity, compassion for people and planet, and profound gratitude. And it is with this profound gratitude, and awe possessing every ounce of our beings, that we fly away from this beloved island that we will call home in nine months. A hui hou.

## Chapter 5: Care

# Cross Country West-East:
# Audre Lorde and Guanyin

*"Caring for myself is not self-indulgence. It is self-preservation and that is an act of political warfare."*
*-Audre Lorde*

We are incredibly stoked to begin the West-East Cross-Country portion of our adventure. After cramming the entire southern half of the country into one month, we're luxuriating in the opportunity to spend a solid four months lingering in national parks and forests throughout the Pacific Northwest, Mountain West, Badlands, and back to the Southeast, the place we called home for so many years. Before this part of the journey can officially begin, however, we will have two weeks of complete stress. Albeit, the stress that comes from beautiful life circumstances, but stress, nevertheless.

**Stress.**

Elizabeth's brother proposed to his girlfriend just before our traveling began, and since they hadn't yet set a date for the wedding, we'd originally planned to fly from Hawai'i to California and begin our big road trip. Once they set the date for April, no distance would keep us away from the celebration, especially since all three of us are slotted to be in the wedding. So, we are flying all the way from Hawai'i to Miami for the nuptials and then flying back to California. Eleven hours of flying and a six-hour time change aren't the easiest with a two-year-old in tow, but we manage. Barely. Riah is actually quite the trooper, and all the grandparents chip in to try and make the situation less stressful once we arrive. The wedding and festivities are beautiful, but since we are the only parents with a young child and the only queer people present, it is a still a little...stressful.

I officiate the wedding. Riah is the ring bearer. And Elizabeth is a bridesmaid, decked out in a lacy pink dress. Let the record show this is probably the third time I've ever seen Elizabeth in a dress in our nearly-decade-long relationship. She looks pretty damn hot in her wedge heels, but she certainly does not feel like herself as we take turns chasing our wild child before and after the ceremony. It's possible that, at one point, Riah hid behind a curtain and threw a dinner roll at an unexpecting table of twentysomethings. I can't quite remember. Did I mention the stress?

Though it is an honor to officiate my brother-in-law's wedding, and both sets of grandparents are going out of their way to host us and help us with Riah, I can't help but feel like a queer outsider looking into a heteronormative celebration of gender roles. Hear this clearly. It's not just Elizabeth's family. Almost all weddings irk me in this way. It's such a celebration of excess riddled with antiquated and patriarchal symbolism. Whether it's the historical reasons for having bridesmaids: so that the groom can marry the next in line should the bride kick the bucket. Or the initial ownership embedded in placing a ring on a woman's finger to symbolize that the man literally owned her as property. Or the "giving away" of the bride from father to groom. This is one place where I've always put my foot down as an officiant. The bride is not a transfer of property from a father to a groom; that's antiquated, oppressive, and gross. I use a ritual I've created called the "Blessing of the Parents" instead. I don't fault her family for engaging all these traditions because they're lifted up as the ideal for girls throughout the country. But my queer feminist heart pounds throughout it all.

After all the effort I put into to crafting a meaningful ceremony for them, the wedding ends, and everyone is kind, appreciative, and complimentary of the ritual I provided by officiating. Then it is time for photos. Hear this clearly, too. I know it's a stressful time for the bride and groom; there are a lot of details to keep in order, and I certainly couldn't be helpful while chasing our toddler throughout the grounds. They take a few photos with officiant and ring bearer present at the beginning so Riah can go play without having to sit and wait any longer. A thoughtful gesture. When the time comes for the big family photo—the one with all the parents and grandparents and siblings and their spouses—the bride's brother's girlfriend is intentionally invited into the photo while Riah and I play on the sidelines, completely excluded from the family photo.

I know this wasn't intentional. Despite the fact that the missing grandmother, too ill to travel to the wedding, still doesn't even know I exist, or that she has a great grandchild, or that Elizabeth is queer, I am confident that no one in her family purposefully left us out. But that doesn't stop it from hurting. I spent at least twenty hours of time researching and crafting their ceremony; we've flown over 6,000 miles and spent thousands of dollars to be here; and as I watched the photographer invite the entire extended family to smile for the camera while my child and I watched in our wedding attire, my eyes welled with tears. This wedding isn't about me or my family. I know this. But it's not just the accidental exclusion from the photo. It's years of all those other exclusions and microaggressions society, family, and church have thrown at us that puddle in my eyes. I feel like such an outsider.

## Sister Outsider.

And I can't help but think of the Sister Outsider who knows even more deeply what it's like to look in from the outside: Audre Lorde. This queer womanist writer and civil rights activist described herself as a "black, lesbian, mother, warrior, poet." In fact, Lorde's 1984 collection of nonfiction prose, *Sister Outsider: Essays and Speeches*, has become a canonical text in women's studies, Black studies, and queer theory. It was reading her that first opened my eyes to my own white privilege and the ways I've contributed to women of color feeling like outsiders.

Lorde dedicated her entire life and all her writing and creative talent to confronting the intersecting injustices of racism, sexism, classism, and homophobia. She earned a BA from Hunter College and MLS from Columbia, serving as a librarian in the New York public school system throughout the 1960s. It was here that she met her husband, a white, gay man with whom she had two children. Living more fully into her authentic self, she met her long-time partner (wife was not a term afforded to her during her lifetime), Frances Clayton.

She taught poetry and writing, and created a pedagogy based on her experience as a black, queer woman in white academia. Her essay, "The Master's Tools Will Not Dismantle the Master's House" remains a foundational text in my own classroom, and in countless classrooms grappling with critical theories addressing gender, sexuality, and race. She is often quoted within the recent self-care movement for claiming, "Caring for myself is not self-indulgence. It is self-preservation and that is an act of political warfare." And, while this statement stands solid on its own, I think it's imperative to utilize her work on self-care through the lens of her Sister

Outsider status. She wasn't just talking about self-care as bubble baths and a spa day. She was talking about radical self-care for collective liberation. I liken this to an analogy Elizabeth has often employed to describe the work we do as we envision empowerment differently. Given our lesbionic tendencies, it involves power tools. Stick with me.

If your power saw doesn't work, there are typically one of three things wrong:

1. the blade is too dull and needs either sharpening or replacement,
2. your battery is drained and needs charging, or
3. your power source is faulty and won't adequately charge your battery.

So it is with empowerment work. Most women's empowerment work—in ministry, entrepreneurship, art, spirituality—focus only on the first two issues. With "blade sharpening," we're taught to change our perspective and behaviors: be mindful, work harder, meditate, pray, or exercise. AKA sharpen our blades. And this important. So, we go on yoga or meditation retreats, take classes, and discipline ourselves. With "drained batteries" the analogy is obvious: self-care and recharge. We're encouraged to sleep more, take a bubble bath, go to a spa, or drink a glass of wine. This is also important. Mindfulness and bubble baths are lovely, but blade sharpening and recharging batteries aren't enough to empower marginalized women.

Rather, we need to also examine our power sources. We live in a culture where power sources are structurally designed to disenfranchise women and marginalized communities, from the pulpit to the academy, board room to public office. And if we blade sharpen and recharge, but still find ourselves exhausted or overwhelmed, we're made to feel as though *we* are the problem. We're faulty or not working hard enough. But the problem isn't us. It's the power systems that ignore, exclude, or malign us and our work. No meditation or spa day can fix that. So, we endeavor to do all three simultaneously. Yes, we blade sharpen by painting and writing, rituals, meditation, yoga, exercise, and doing the Examen. Yes, we try to find time to recharge with playfulness, rest, sleep, and a glass of wine. But we also acknowledge and examine the power structures that tear us down, so that we can be galvanized to subvert and dismantle them. This is the care Audre Lorde speaks of.

In Miami, I don't have the energy to dismantle. I hug my child. I kiss my wife. I cling to the worth of our family, photo or no photo. And then we are invited inside the circle. As we eat dinner and dance with Riah at the reception, Elizabeth's stepfather pulls us aside. He is a gentle man with a kind heart; he reminds me of Mr. Rogers. He gives us each a hug, looks us both in the eye, and says, "This has been a beautiful wedding, and I'm glad you came all the way here. I imagine it must be very hard for you because you never got to have a big celebration of your love like this with family and friends. And that's not fair. I felt it was important to acknowledge that."

Then, as we are packing up to leave the wedding, Elizabeth's dad resolutely informs her, "As you know, it's customary for the groom's parents to pay for the rehearsal dinner." He then tells her how much he paid for the rehearsal. "Well, you and Angela never got to have a celebration like this, so I'm going to give you the same amount of money. You can put it toward all you're creating in Hawai'i. My children deserve to be treated equally."

Sister outsiders we remain, but sometimes we are invited into the circle by men trying their best to be accomplices in the queer feminist work we do. After the wedding, we fly back to California. Six hours and several time zones later, we pick up our Explorer and pop-up camper from generous former congregants who have graciously stored it for us, and set up camp in the parking lot of the church where I was an Associate Pastor for Arts and Education for five years. Fly from Hawai'i to Miami, officiate a wedding, fly from Miami to California, and set up camp in less than two weeks. With a two-year-old. Seriously. We are finally officially ready to begin the cross-country adventure of our dreams with the care Audre Lorde has emboldened within us.

**Daddy.**

Elizabeth has secured the first of many free campgrounds, thus providing us time to plan, and take a moment to breathe before four months of slow travel. Unlike the other boondocking places she has found along our route, this free campground comes with a catch. The location is lovely, nestled between Napa Valley and Sacramento with rolling hills that are on the cusp of changing from green to golden. The actual campground is stocked with amenities, the things we usually forego in search of solitude and scenery: pool, restaurant, clubhouse, kid camps. To camp for free at this amenity-rich location—plush with hook ups for water, electric, and wi-fi—means that you have to attend their sales pitch for a time share. The pitch, they assured, would take less than ninety minutes. So, we hook up the camper and schedule a time with one of their sales associates. No matter what is said or done during the ninety-minute sales pitch, it will be worth the $250 we are saving to camp there for four nights. Plus, there is free wine and cookies.

The pitch isn't that bad, and it would probably make sense for a family that lived nearby and wanted to vacation at this campground on the regular, while also receiving discounts at approved locations throughout the country. But we're not that family and likely won't return to camp outside of Sacramento anytime soon. The problem is not with the pitch, but with the salesman. We knew when we booked the location that our queerness could be an issue. Having lived in Berkeley and Oakland for five years, we experienced glimpses of the radical welcome California had to offer, but we also knew that other parts of the state weren't so open-minded. When a troop of middle-aged lesbians guided us as we backed up Little Freya, we looked around and realized we were in the total gayborhood of the campground. With this is mind, we enter the sales pitch with eased minds. Until we meet the salesman.

Like many of the men who showed or sold us campers, this dude seems completely perplexed by our family, asking the nature of our relationship numerous times, even though he repeatedly hears Riah call us mommy and mama. When he learns that I'm an author and professor, his pitch derails as he asked for help in publishing a book. When I request that we focus on the pitch, he notes that I probably wouldn't be helpful since professors don't own the intellectual property of their books and all rights go to the university. This is not even close to true, but I don't want to add to the ninety minutes, so I simply steer him back to camping.

Then it happens for the first time.

"Daddy."

He calls Elizabeth, "daddy." We exchange confused and annoyed looks. The salesman continues. He hands Riah a coloring page and crayons to entertain him for the remainder of the pitch and says, "Why don't you color a nice picture for daddy," while gesturing to Elizabeth. Our eyes grow wide as we exchange another set of perplexed looks.

"Yes, Riah, do you want to use *mommy's* favorite color, green?" I say to Riah, placing extreme emphasis on the fact that Riah calls Elizabeth mommy.
Elizabeth adds, "Or would you like to use *mama's* favorite color, yellow?"
We've made it abundantly clear on several occasions that Riah calls us mommy and mama, and the salesman has heard Riah use these parental terms. Nevertheless, he persists in calling Elizabeth "daddy" throughout the entire ninety minutes, despite our corrections.

We leave annoyed, insulted, invalidated, but mostly laughing at this guy's complete ineptitude in grasping our family, appropriateness, or professionalism. There is no way in hell we are going to buy into their camping timeshare plan, especially after dealing with this unaware mansplainer, but we are so overwhelmed by his brazen obtuseness that we simply tell him we'd think about it and get back to him the next day.

Hear this clearly. There is absolutely nothing wrong with a queer parent using the title "daddy" in their parenting. I know of a lot of queer women who opt to use gender neutral parental names, or ones traditionally associated with men. Nothing wrong with that. Dismantle the binary. Reconstruct life-giving language. Rage against the status quo. The problem is that this bonehead ignored the fact that Riah and I repeatedly called Elizabeth "mommy" and that there was absolutely no one in our family named "daddy." What the hell, man?

After discussing it together, we decide that I should broach the topic with him, offer a constructive corrective, and tell the oblivious salesman that we do not want the timeshare. I prepare my words carefully in my mind and walk to his office with confidence, knowing that I can stand up for myself and my family in the same way that I have taught my students and congregants to do. This confidence is derailed by the salesman. Before I can utter a word, he informs me that he's thought a lot about the books I've published and determined that I need a lesson from a salesman in how to better market them. He then launches into how *he* could better market and sell my books than my publishers could. I am completely flabbergasted. This ass-hat was asking me for publishing advice only one day prior. He is not a writer. He has no expertise in my field. He has never published anything. And he spent the evening referring to my wife as "daddy." I simply tell him the same thing we tell Riah to say whenever someone says or does something you don't like. "No thanks." And I walk away.

In hindsight, I've thought of so many better responses, ranging from thoughtful and instructive to assailing and snarky. The salesman needs to learn that it's not appropriate to refer to people—and queer people in particular—with words they have not chosen for themselves, that it's important to listen to the terms people use for themselves and their families and simply repeat those terms. And normally, I'm a pretty damn good teacher, not just calling out, but calling into awareness with grace and dignity and intentional instruction. But it's not my fucking job to teach this dude what words to use. Get a clue, man!

There have been several times since leaving those rolling hills that I've considered calling the campground and setting the record straight (or gay, rather). But it's so emotionally draining and invalidating that I don't bother; instead, emboldened by Audre Lorde, I nestle into my own self-care. Not a time has passed by when I've referred to Elizabeth as "daddy" that we haven't burst into hysterical laughter, though. So, there's that.

**The Rock.**

From Daddy's campground, we head north, playing in Mount Shasta and then relishing our propane-fed heater as we dry camp (no electric or water) in Crater Lake where there is 6 feet of snow! We figure that, since we just spent the entire winter in bikinis, we can probably handle a few days of snow. From Crater Lake, we continue to free camp in Eugene, where we savor some delicious vegan food, enjoy long runs along the river, and battle epic allergies. When purchasing allergy medication, I learn that Eugene is the allergy capital of the country. Who knew?

The most stunning stop is sans electric, water, Wi-Fi, or cell service in the Clatsop State Forest outside of Portland, where we enjoy a beautiful campsite, a stunning Tolkienesque hike along the ridge dripping with verdant mosses and ferns, and awe-inspiring views while doing outdoor yoga. Though we have settled into a camper parking and driving routine that suits each of our skills, we have inadvertently switched roles at Clatsop after a sleazy dude threatened Elizabeth and made her anxious at the gas station. Usually, Elizabeth drives in tight campgrounds and I drive on the freeway; we each get too anxious doing the opposite. Similarly, Elizabeth *always* backs up the camper, and I *always* direct. If I attempt to back up, we inevitably go in the wrong direction, and if Elizabeth tries to direct me, she ends up waving her arms like Grover from Sesame Street and muttering incomprehensibly. We learned this the hard way while I tried to do a simple back up in California and ended up scraping off a little part of the camper on a tree.

Since there is no official check in spot in Clatsop, I don't need to hop out and register while a host tells me to inform my "husband" to back up, all while Elizabeth tucks into the driver's side. The roads seem wide enough for me to handle driving through the campground loop. Nope. I curve around a U as we both realize I am a bit too close to the large boulders outlining the edge of the campground. Elizabeth hops out to direct me. Why we don't switch roles, I do not know. She flails her gangly arms and mutters something incomprehensible, I lurch backward, turning the steering wheel in the completely wrong direction. She flails. I lurch. She hollers. I roll down the window to shout, "huh?" Riah adds his own directions from the back seat: "cut, left, a little more, three feet, right, you got it. Nice job, mama!" Elizabeth sprints to the driver's side window. "You're stuck on a rock," she informs me. "What?!" I cry.

Hopping out of the driver's side door, my eyes behold, not a rock, but an enormous boulder, somewhere between the size of a miniature pony and a mini cooper. My eyes grow wide. "How in the hell did we do that?" I cry. "Why didn't you tell me I was so close?" I ask Elizabeth. "I did," she informs me, illustrating with Grover arms and an indecipherable mumble. We lock eyes in that moment where most couples would dig into a major argument. Fortunately, we're the type of communicators that don't see the point in arguing over something that clearly will not fix the problem. We burst into laughter as Riah begs from the car seat, "Funny joke, mama? What's so funny, mommy?" We agree to stick to our skillsets in the future and swap roles, Elizabeth driving and me directing. There is no directing and no backing off this rock, though. We manage to wedge Little Freya even firmer onto the boulder. Ooops.

Unbuckling Riah from the car seat, we sheepishly set off to ask for help. I tell someone roasting marshmallows of our dilemma, mortified that we two women had to ask a burly man to aid us, thereby setting the example that

113

women the world over are incapable of driving campers. What a burden to represent the masses in this way.

He is generous, kind, helpful, and completely baffled at how exactly we managed to get our camper stuck atop such a massive boulder. Inviting another man to help, they pull out all their tools, jack up the camper, remove a wheel, put the wheel back on, and get us off the rock. After successfully parking under a moss laden tree by the river, I dash back to the nearest gas station to buy them cookies and beer as a thank you gift. Never again will I attempt to back up. And never again will Elizabeth try directing. It's worth noting that we never got stuck on another rock, either.

**Wrecked.**

After Elizabeth has found us so many free stops, we need to pause long enough to use a real dump station and charge the camper's batteries. We pause for a splurge night at the swankiest of swank campgrounds: a luxury KOA bordering Washington State. We set up camp, surrounded by azaleas, amenities, rhododendron, and rich people. Then I begin receiving texts from my mom to call her. This is out of the ordinary. She never wants to inconvenience anyone, so she would only ask someone to call if it was an emergency. My mind races as I call, certain that Carl has died, that she's discovered he was addicted to drugs again, and that meth or alcohol has ended his life.

Sitting on a kelly green picnic table next to our camper in Astoria, I brace myself for meth, heroin, cocaine. Carl finally had opened up enough to say he had spent most of his savings and was having trouble sleeping. He denied any drug use. My mom said he was welcome to sleep at her place, concerned that staying in his apartment alone may be depressing him. He stayed late into the evening after my mom had fallen sleep. She awoke to a strange rattling noise in the living room and walked in to find Carl passed out on her sofa with a can of computer duster in his hand. Beside him was a duffle bag filled with cans of duster.

His secret out in the open, Carl admitted that he had spent all his savings— over $20,000—on computer duster. Despite research to the contrary, he insisted it wasn't harmful or addictive. The reality is that every time a person huffs duster, they are playing Russian roulette. There are instances of people dying the first time they inhale it; it's called Sudden Sniffing

114

Death. Even though duster cans provide ample warning labels, it is not regulated; it doesn't show up on a drug test; and you can buy it almost anywhere. And that's precisely what Carl was doing. He hadn't exactly lied to us because he wasn't technically doing drugs because duster isn't considered a drug.

My mom puts Carl on the line. He tells us he wants to get better, that he needs help. But he refuses rehab because the only rehab facilities we can afford are faith-based non-profits that utilize a twelve-step program. He disagrees with both.

I can't blame him for this. I'm afraid. I sit on the fucking picnic table at the fancy campground over three thousand miles away from my little brother. Completely helpless. I crumple to the ground, the smell of freshly cut grass engulfing my face as I breathe deeply, imagining the sensation he had every time he breathed in the bitter taste of duster.

I need to process. I truncate the story for Elizabeth and put on my running shoes. I have to get out of my head and into my body. Without a destination in mind, I hit one of the trails leading to the ocean and run hard, sweat and tears finding common ground on my face as I heave toward the Pacific. Rounding a wide curve, the classic Pacific Northwest forest begins to part. I squint as the sun bounces off shiny metal. Sand slows my pace as I come face-to-face with an abandoned shipwreck. Expansive sand flattened and absorbed the weight of metal framing. Water pooled around the edges. Children splashed and tourists took photos. Surely, they came knowing what to expect. The signage, I later noticed, clearly indicated that this was "Shipwreck Beach." But I hadn't seen the signs or chosen this beach. I'd just come to charge my camper's battery and use the dump station. A phone call on a picnic table changed everything.

I stand in front of the shipwreck, not knowing why or how it got there, not pausing to read the signs. With sweat pouring over my body, I think of nothing but Carl. About how many of his brilliant braincells were now dead, dusted away for a high. About the beauty we tried to fill his life with when my father's addiction, divorce, bullying, poverty, and random acts of violence otherwise gave him nothing but shit. Am I looking for signs? Because one is right in front of me. A life and a ship, wrecked.

**More Shit.**

Though Carl refused my offer to come back to help in person, there isn't much I can actually do from so far away. I research rehab facilities and reach out to my network in Atlanta, but he refuses any mental health care, and no matter how much you love someone, you can't force them to get help. As we slowly truck north, I continue to ponder an ethic of care and how Lorde would care for herself and my brother amid this cycle of addiction.

After a stunning time in Olympic National Park–trail running on the magical Hoh and soaking up the sights at Ruby Beach–we begin the long journey eastward. Though Elizabeth has spent some time in the Mountain West during winter, it is my first time in this part of the country, and we savor every drop of beauty in Idaho, Montana, and Wyoming. Our first stop is Glacier National Park, where we have about 72 hours of non-stop rain and freezing temps, but that doesn't stop us from catching the jaw dropping views when the rain stops. We have sunny skies once we arrive on the east side of the park, where the amazing views, bear-spray-laden hikes, alpine lakes, and snow-capped mountains never cease to take our breath away.

After placing one of Riah's poop diapers just outside the camper door in Glacier long enough for me to change his pants and wash my hands, there is a steady rapping at Little Freya's door. I open it to see the campground host, clad in a tucked-in volunteer National Parks t-shirt, fanny pack, and ranger hat. A stern look tightens her face and her finger aims downward at Riah's poop diaper. "What's this?" she implores, rigidly.
"My toddler just pooped. I was going to take it to the grizzly safe trash bins once I finished cleaning up," I inform her.
"Human waste attracts bears," she proclaims through gritted teeth.
"I'm sorry," I mutter, "it's literally been sitting there less than two minutes."
"Nevertheless," she cries, finger pointing toward the crisp, blue sky.
"Ok, I'll take it over," I mutter, beginning to close the door so I could finish putting on Riah's pants and shoes before picking up the diaper that was tempting grizzlies throughout the park to indulge in a fetid amuse-bouche before devouring my tiny child. The campground host wraps her fingers around the closing door, flings it wide, and jabs her finger, once again, at the poop laden diaper. Her eyebrow raises, reminding me of the strictest of elementary school teachers. So, I perch my pantsless, shoeless child on my hip, pick up the wretched grizzly temptation and carry it to the

lockable trash bins. I can't help but think of all the midnight diapers dropped outside our door, intent on a morning trashcan delivery in Vermont and Virginia, or that embarrassing bag full of my own poop tied snuggly one rainy summer night. Perhaps brown bears don't have the appetite for food that has already made its way through the digestive track in the same way grizzlies do.

## Cycles.

As the snow-capped mountains of Glacier fade in our rearview mirror, I find out that Carl has been evicted. Our youngest brother, Josh, went to Carl's apartment to help him pack and found thousands of cans of duster filling his apartment. Carl insisted on cleaning it on his own, hauling enormous trash bags overflowing with duster cans to the dumpster while Josh sat on the curb, offering to help haul every time Carl passed. "If you want to help, give me the keys to the truck," Carl told him. Josh asked him where he planned to go, knowing that he'd already totaled a car and driven while high. Carl ignored the question and went back hauling trash bags. When Josh looked the other way, Carl snatched the keys out of his hand, jumped in the truck, flicked him off, and sped away.

Thirty minutes later, the truck squealed into the parking lot and Carl stumbled out, high as a kite, duster cans rolling out the driver's side door. The apartment emptied, Josh drove Carl to move in with my mom, and then joined our dad on a motorcycle trip across the country to meet up with my queer little family in Yellowstone and the Tetons. Josh was on his own journey of becoming after camping through Hawai'i and now joining us on his motorcycle. Like Carl, he'd battled addiction in his younger years. Car wrecks, drugs, arrests, probation, dead-end jobs, depression, and poverty ruled much of their lives. The difference was that Josh decided to embrace a resilience and search for what he truly wanted to do, to heal. He even read Audre Lorde. Josh invited his family into his journey and welcomed help and advice. Carl just won't let us in. I know he must feel so lonely, like an outsider himself.

Countless studies show that the primary factor leading to addiction isn't actually drugs or disposition, but ACE: Adverse Childhood Experience. According the to CDC, ACEs are traumatic events that occur within childhood and adolescence, such as experiencing violence, abuse, or neglect, death of loved ones, parental substance abuse, mental health problems, instability, parental separation or divorce, incarceration, poverty, etc. There is a survey that assesses one's ACE on a scale of 1-10. Anyone with an ACE of 4 nearly doubles the risk of heart disease and cancer, increases the likelihood of becoming an alcoholic by 700 percent and the risk of attempted suicide by 1200 percent. My brother never had the opportunity to take this survey. But I took it for myself and on his behalf, which could potentially exclude some of his trauma that I was never aware of. We both have an ACE of 7.

So, the question is not, "Why is Carl doing this to himself? Why is he an addict?" It's "How have I avoided this thus far? Why am I *not* an addict?" One doctor, Daniell Sumrok, doesn't even believe addiction should be called "addiction," but "ritualized compulsive comfort-seeking." This comfort-seeking, according to Sumrok, is a normal response to trauma, just like bleeding is a normal response to being cut. If only society could embrace Audre Lorde's ethic of care as a response rather than demonizing addicts and the mentally ill.

Let me be clear in saying that my brothers and I have an absolutely amazing mother who showered us with love in abundance, doing the best she could as a single working mom without higher education or a support network. But having an addict for a father partnered with violence born of poverty meant my little brother experienced a hell of a lot of trauma before he even finished elementary school. And my father's ACE is even higher than ours. Cycles of addiction, poverty, and neglect are hard to break. I feel so helpless.

Spring fades to summer as our little camper chugs through the country. Yellowstone impresses us more than we thought it would. Between bison, wolves, deer, elk, bear, fumeroles, hot springs, mud pots, waterfalls, and canyons, we are constantly amazed. After one day on our own in Yellowstone, my dad and Josh arrive on their motorcycles, pitching tents by our camper.

I relish the opportunity to climb 8,500 feet and do a big hike with Josh, as we filled our hats with melting snow to assuage the sweat and burn in our thighs. Soaking in the sheer beauty and magic of getting to spend some quality time with my youngest brother, our conversation inevitably turns to Carl. Neither of us know what to do, and Josh has been increasingly concerned about the toll it is taking on our mom, as am I. After spotting grizzlies in the distance toward the end of our hike, we find a spot in the park with free hot showers. These showers are amazing and stocked with the best smelling soaps. We each indulge in long, hot showers to wash away the sweat of the hike and the filth of weeks camping without running water. Wet-haired and wafting the sent of fresh rosemary and cucumber, we sit in the sun with ice cream cones in our grateful hands.

Upon returning to the campsite, my dad and Josh offer to watch Riah the next evening so that Elizabeth and I can have a blessed date night. We haven't had one of those since dad visited us in Hawai'i, so we cannot be more excited. After a morning of all five of us hiking together, Elizabeth and I set off on our date. It begins with another luxurious free, hot shower. Then we do a short hike at Pallette Springs, and my phone rings just as we are deciding on where to eat dinner. It is my mom. As bison amble past, I immediately answer, confident the call is about Carl.

He totaled her car after lying and using grocery money she gave him on duster. Mom is in tears. My mother is amazingly strong and resilient. She raised us as a single working parent living below the poverty line, and never complained throughout our childhood or adolescence. She battled breast cancer like a champ, and always taught the three of us the importance of having a positive attitude and working hard no matter what life throws at you. My empathy for Carl is transforming into rage at the way he is treating our mom. She hands her cell to him and asks him to please talk to me.

Carl tells me he truly wants to get better, that he knows he can't do it on his own, that he doesn't want to treat his family this way. It sounds like he begins to cry, but he doesn't have functioning tear ducts, so he literally cannot cry. I've often wondered if this was some kind of physiological manifestation of Carl's innerworkings. He felt deeply, I could tell, but he would never let his emotions out, or invite anyone else in. As a very young child he did, but then he began to be bullied at school.

In the first grade, teenagers broke into the project complex we lived in when he was home alone and tried to slit his throat. Only months later, he was jumped while riding his bike home from school as kids tore apart the paper bag holding his books; his backpack had been previously stolen. As a middle schooler, he was jumped on Halloween and beaten with a padlock as teenagers ran away with his candy. And he was bullied so much for being fat in high school that he chose to drop out rather than deal with teenagers' shit. There was personal responsibility he had to own up to, but there were some pretty systemic problems that disenfranchised his ability to get the help he needed.

Poverty. Toxic masculinity that teaches men that the only appropriate emotions are lust and anger. The remnants of the war on drugs. A broken criminal justice system. A society that demonizes addiction. Unaffordable and inaccessible healthcare that treats addicts like criminals. A culture that demonizes mental illness. Even as a straight, white, man, these systems have failed him. As the deer, bison, and tourists saunter past and I listen to my brother, I can't think about all those systems, though. All I can think about is how pissed off at him I am for hurting my mom so much, my mom who has and would go to the moon to help her children. I tell him about all my contacts in Atlanta who could help, all the treatment facilities I could help him into. I tell him how much I love him, how I want him to heal and live, and to stop killing himself and our mom.

We hang up the phone and Elizabeth and I finish our date. I am angry and forlorn. I am selfishly resentful that one of the few times I could spend alone with my wife has been hampered by my brother's bullshit. It's so fucking hard to love an addict, and it's even harder to help them when they don't want help at all.

From Yellowstone, we make the short drive to Grand Teton National Park and the adorable town of Jackson, WY. The hike to Taggart Lake takes the cake in the Tetons. With the mountains reflected in the lake and a vibrant forest surrounding us, all five of us are awestruck. The homesteads are spectacular, too. And we are quite taken with the town of Jackson Hole, which manages to offer all the things you'd need with beauty and without the kitsch of most tourist areas. With several vegan restaurants, Josh and dad offer to give us another date night, which we happily accept. Over samosas I receive another call from my mom.

Carl stole her credit card to buy duster, and was now refusing to go to rehab, despite promising her otherwise. She is reaching the end of her rope. My cousin's husband had spent a year of in-house rehab with the Salvation Army and had risked a lot to recommend Carl for a spot there. Though the Salvation Army has a horrible reputation for their treatment of queer people, this treatment program saved his life. Because it was faith-based and rooted in the twelve-step program, however, Carl wouldn't even go to the meetings. Elizabeth and I end our date brainstorming ways to help my brother again.

**Community.**

As our time in the Tetons comes to a close, I begin to long for my faith community and community organizing, not so much for faith or spirituality, but for the support that comes with a community gathered around justice issues in solidarity, lamentation, and outrage. The kind that gives you hope when your heart is heavy from laughably offensive rulings in rape cases at Stanford and hate massacres of fellow queers in Orlando.

As the rapist Brock Turner is given a slap on the wrist for penetrating an unconscious woman behind a dumpster at Stanford, the two sexual assaults I experienced in high school and college trigger my wandering heart. I feel angry, afraid, enraged at the way women's bodies are treated, at the way my own body has been treated at the hands of sexually toxic men. And then there is Pulse.

On June 12, 2016 Omar Mateen massacres forty-nine people at Pulse, a gay night club in Orlando that was hosting Latin night. It is the largest mass shooting since Wounded Knee, clearly a hate crime aimed at queer people of color. As the news progresses, I am glued to my social media feeds, checking in on members of my former LGBTQ Spirituality Group, reaching out to friends and clergy in Florida, and feeling my sense of security and safety silently waft farther and farther out of grasp. My queer little family mourns. We grieve. I weep. And fear. And rage. When I was a pastor, or connected with the clergy in the community organizing group I was part of in North Carolina, I had had a beloved community with whom to grieve, offer and find support. Together, we would have organized a vigil or a protest or some kind of communal ritual to provide space for lamentation, grief, and healing. Flailing, I contact some of the local progressive faith communities in Jackson Hole, but no one is doing or planning anything. In those hours and days following the shooting, I need the communities I have left behind. I long to don my clergy collar, hold a candle, and sing alongside queer kindred and fellow activists from the black churches in town, "We Shall Overcome." This is the first time I have yearned to be part of the tradition I no longer call my own. Not for faith or religion or spirituality, but for solidarity. To know I'm not grieving this alone.

121

**Recall.**

On the heels of these events, our hearts feel heavy. As a woman, a queer woman, a queer woman with Mexican family, I feel vulnerable and emotionally drained. Our little family loads up the camper—like we always do—bidding farewell to my dad and brother and leave the Tetons. The plan is to spend four or five days meandering through Wyoming before arriving at an amazing community housing in Fort Collins, CO. These plans are interrupted by a Ford recall on the Togwotee Pass. I'd never heard of the Togwotee Pass, and to be perfectly honest, I didn't quite realize we were driving on it. It's stunningly beautiful, with sweeping views of the Tetons, fields of wildflowers, and grizzly bear warnings every few miles. It's also tremendously steep. Our little Explorer has the towing package of a semi (hyperbole, but you get the idea), but it still has the V6 engine of a standard Explorer. Recently, Ford recalled the thermostat housing unit, along with the attached sensor. We did not know this since our particular 2004 Explorer has had quite a few owners before us and our trusty Little Freya. So, as we chug our way up the Togwotee Pass, the engine is overheating, and we have no idea because the sensor isn't communicating this important information to us. Because the thermostat housing unit is now cracked— also unbeknownst to us—water is spewing all over the engine. You don't have to be a mechanic to know this is all very bad.

The Check Gauge light comes on just in time for me to pull into the turn lane in front of Togwotee Lodge and Gas Station. As I complete the lane change, the car shuts down and begins smoking. Bad news. Good timing. We get Riah out of the car as fast as possible and look like wild women running across the road. Once the smoke abates, I pop the hood to let it cool long enough so that I can pull it into the parking lot. Until then, the smoking car and attached camper had been sitting in the middle of the Togwotee Pass as two frantic moms tried to remain calm enough not to startle their child.

I call my dad, then on his way toward Utah on his motorcycle. Within moments of learning what had happened, dad and Josh change their plans and ride their motorcycles toward the Pass. In the meantime, I explore the very soaked engine as several people from Togwotee Lodge's maintenance department come out to help. We Google stuff and discover the recall. Everyone agrees that the recall also likely damaged the water pump and it needed to be replaced. Luckily, it's a relatively easy fix, so dad picked up a pump on his way through Jackson and the people at Togwotee spread out the red carpet of welcome.

First, they invite us to stay the night in our camper on their grounds for free. Then they clear out the shop, which was otherwise filled with snow mobiles, and share their tools. Dad and Josh arrive. I treat them to dinner at the lodge and a room, which are well deserved after rerouting their trip to help us. The next day, several folks help my dad replace the water pump while we hike through stunning trails and spot a mama deer followed by a newly born fawn. It is so tiny it looks like a puppy. We agree this was a fortunate place to break down.

The time comes for the inaugural test drive. Dad selects a beautiful spot to pull over to admire the Tetons and take photos. And then we are inundated with white smoke. Dad shakes his head. "I was worried this would happen," he sighs. Head gaskets are blown. Fixing this involves nearly gutting the entire engine. In a full shop it would take at least three days (in the middle of the woods without proper tools it takes eight). And in Jackson it would cost over $3,000, plus the cost of towing down the pass for fifty miles. This is really not good.

Another kind stranger emerges through the smoke. He sniffs. "Head gaskets?" he asks. Dad nods solemnly. "What can I do to tell help?" the stranger offers. A beautiful conversation ensues. Recommendations are made. And I hop into the stranger's car to go back to the lodge with the soymilk I had mistakenly forgotten to leave for Riah just before naptime. The stranger-now-friend drops me off with my little family, fills three-gallon jugs with water, and buys antifreeze on the sly so that I won't offer to pay for it. He returns to my dad, along with a couple other people from the lodge, also laden with water and antifreeze. No one had to do these things. They just did. Everyone keeps saying, "We know how hard it is to be stuck."

The maintenance and general manager of the lodge help us haul the camper to an out-of-the-way spot, plugs us into power and tells us to take as long as we need. This is a nice lodge. The kind of lodge where rooms are over $250 per night. The cabins are even more. They probably don't want people sleeping in campers and their car—which is precisely what my generous dad and brother are planning—for a total of eight days. But they invite us to do this, asking nothing in return. When I slump past the front desk to fill up my water bottle, someone hands me a chocolate bar and says, "You probably need this." As I drown my sorrows in chocolate, the bartender leaves the Saloon and sits beside me. "Broken head gaskets need tequila shots," she tells me. Together, we toast. And it is good, smooth tequila.

For eight days, my dad and brother work tirelessly on the car. They ride their motorcycles into town—a five-hour round trip—to pick up parts that sometimes don't arrive on time. And then they drive back the next day. The staff at Togwotee unlock showers for us so we can bathe, help on the car during their breaks, give us directions to secret hikes, drive to pick us up propane so that we can have heat at night, comp one of our meals, and extend an exorbitantly generous amount of hospitality. We keep Riah busy with stunning hikes and WiFi-streamed episodes of Daniel Tiger. We see wildflower meadows and snow-capped mountains, baby moose and elk. They celebrate with us when the engine turns for the first time, and when the car runs, and when the subsequent fuel leak is fixed. It is grace and beauty and hospitality and kindness comingling in one of the most stunning places we've visited this year. We agree, once again, that this was a fortunate place to break down.

After several test drives, we determine that the car is safe to continue our pilgrimage. Hitched and ready, we bid our beloved Togwotee farewell, drop off a thick stack of Thank You cards, and whiten our knuckles as we drive the rest of the way up the Pass. Dad and Josh plan to follow on the motorcycles to our first stop…just in case. We arrive, set up camp, go to the grocery store, and they are still nowhere to be found. Without cell service along the Pass, I begin to worry. Finally, I hear from Josh. His motorcycle had a flat tire. Can they not get a break?! What follows was another hilarious night of Wyoming hospitality. We are fine. They are fine. After over three weeks together, our ways have parted.

The next day we break down outside of Laramie, WY. We overheated. This is not good. With lots of water, I get us close enough to call AAA and get towed. A gracious tow truck driver and mechanic go above and beyond by towing us, dropping us off at a restaurant for dinner, and then insisting that we simply set up camp in the back lot behind the shop. Later, he shows up with 21 gallons of water to fill the camper and a back-up generator in case we need power. Flanked by two rusted semis, we swat mosquitoes as bunnies hop through old car parts.

That night we struggle to fall asleep. Elizabeth reminds me that Laramie is the town where Matthew Shephard was beaten, tortured, and strung to a fence to die. All because he was gay. I think of the generous mechanic who has lived in Laramie his entire life. He lived here when Matthew Shephard was left to die. He had extended hospitality to two queer women and their child. Did he realize that we're gay? Did he care? Does it matter? With Orlando and Stanford and Shephard on my mind, I feel afraid and grateful at the same time. Grateful for overwhelming hospitality. Afraid that the safety we often feel as queer traveling women with a young child is an illusion. One in three women are raped or sexually assaulted at least once within a lifetime. Two live in our camper. Queer bodies are attacked, legislated, violated, killed, and still preachers and politicians purport that our lives and loves and bodies are abominations unworthy of acceptance, celebration, worth. The semis in the dusty gravel lot cast eerie shadows. Trains whistle a little too loudly. Riah crawls into our bed after a declaring that he has had a bad dream. Sleep eludes me.

The next morning, I run through the dilapidated town to clear my head. I return to learn that the head gaskets have blown again. The lower part of the engine is now likely damaged. It's time to bid our beloved Explorer farewell. It is June 26, 2016. Exactly one year prior, we'd left on this wild adventure with a green canoe strapped to the top of the Explorer, dragging a pop-up camper in the direction of Vermont. She has served us well. As we call dealerships, negotiated prices, and researched towing power, I think about my privileges. I think of my fears. I think of the borderlands in which I exist on a daily basis as a white, cisgender, queer woman who is highly educated, but who comes from a poor, working class family who never had the privilege of higher education.

I think about how I spent over a decade privileging myself with degrees, knowledge, and the ability to navigate harrowing situations, while simultaneously examining all the existential questions affiliated with them. I think about Orlando and Matthew Shephard and the unconscious woman raped behind a dumpster by a wealthy college athlete who was simply slapped on the wrist with three months in jail.

I think of the way my own body was violated in college and how I thought nothing of it because almost every woman I know has been treated this way. I think of how my poor father could never give me the language to speak in the world in which I now reside as a scholar and author, but he gave me the language to speak to mechanics so that they don't treat me like I'm "just some girl" who knows nothing about cars. These borderlands of difference accompany me, my wife, and our child as a nice car dealership drives up from Cheyenne to tow our car and camper to their lot and sell us a shiny truck to tow Little Freya off into the sunset of our Year of Volunteer Travel Discernment. With privilege dripping from our pores, existential angst seeping from our veins, and hospitality freely given, we drive away hopeful and afraid and grateful. Raging and wondering and wandering through unlikely places of hospitality and beauty. Likely always.

**Shock and Awe.**

After this, our time in Colorado feels like a gift. A moment to breathe and rest. Another queer family is hosting us as we stay in their intentional community. Riah has been able to play with other children. We have WiFi and hot showers. The fabulous food trucks and sprawling parks are an added bonus. From Fort Collins we drive to a campground just outside of Denver as we welcome Riah's birth mom for another visit. Swimming and sandboxes, trampoline parks and views of dilapidated trains fill our days. Then a tornado hits. We can literally see it swirling toward us in the distance. Alarms sound, but virtually everyone in the campground continues with business as usual. We rally into the campground bathroom because it is made of concrete and lacks windows, but we sit in there alone, no one else concerned that a twister might pick up their RV and send them in the direction of Oz. Everything ended up fine, but it was an odd way to end our time with Riah's birth mother.

As Little Freya bounds toward the Dakotas, my mother calls again. She's finally reached her breaking point. She'd promised Josh that he could move in with her months prior, before she had even learned of Carl's addiction, and now the time has come for him to return to Atlanta. Carl stole her credit card again and failed to show up every time he was scheduled to meet with her at a rehab facility. Her blood pressure was through the roof and she'd tried both compassion and tough love to no avail. She told Carl of her profound love for him, that she wanted to help him, but she couldn't if he wouldn't try to help himself. The ultimatum was go to rehab, or move into your dad's house. He moved to dad's.

Our time in South Dakota is profound. Profoundly hot. Profoundly fun. Profoundly meaningful. Rapid City, the Badlands, Wind Cave, Custer State

Park, Sioux Falls, and a tiny town of 800 called Marion with a free campground, flush with electric, water, and a public pool with multiple diving boards. We spend an abundance of time hiking, dry camping on the Wall outside the Badlands surrounded by swaths of sunflowers and curly horned sheep headbutting far too close to the camper for comfort. Clad in water wings, Riah cannonballs into the deep end and loves his goggles so much he sometimes wears them in the car. With Carl cashless at my father's, I'm fairly certain he doesn't use for a while. We begin to worry slightly less, laugh more, and even begin to relax. He talks of a new job opportunity he might take, one where one of his former colleagues recommended him.

From the Dakotas we make our way toward Wisconsin Dells. Now, when we set out to plan two cross-country adventures, Wisconsin Dells was never on our list. In fact, I'd never really heard of it until a dear friend opened a business there during the summer months. Apparently, it has one of the largest collections of amusement parks and water parks in the world. Though large crowds with commercial attractions are definitely not our scene, I didn't want to pass up the opportunity to see my beloved friend, especially now that she'd opened a second business that offered build-your-own vegan pizzas. Spoiler alert: it's delicious!

In the Dells, we opt to forgo all the tourist attractions, but compromise by actually paying for a campground with a pool rather than dry camping for free. As mosquitoes swarm and humidity drips out our pores while setting up camp, my phone rings. Generally, I don't answer if I don't recognize the number because I like neither spam, nor talking on the phone. Given all that was going on with Carl, I answer.
"This is Angela," I intone.
"Hi, Angela, this is Nick from the television show Tiny House Nation. Do you have a moment to talk?"
You. Must. Be. Kidding. Me.

The possibilities begin spiraling quickly. We need to interview and film a pitch online, so we're lucky that the one place we stopped where we had friends happened to be when we received the call. While they want Riah in the pitch for a few moments, they don't want him chattering in the background, so my friend graciously shares her home and blessed WiFi with us, stealing away with Riah in her room, where they watch cartoons and eat copious amounts of strawberries while we finish our interview. They'll get back to us.

When Riah awakes at 5am the next morning, I am so eager that I pop open the jogging stroller and run through the campground. As the sky fills with a magenta sunrise, Riah points into the woods and proclaims, "Chanterelle!" And what to my wandering eyes did appear, but the red chanterelle mushrooms of the late season. We pick and run, spy more and pick, as my run turns into more of a frolic. "We're moving to Hawai'i to create our dream, and we're going to build an off-grid sustainable tiny house, and Tiny House Nation is probably going to build it, and 5 million people will learn about the work of the Tehom Center non-profit," I think as I sauté chanterelles with onions, garlic, and pole beans. Is this real life?

The calls, interviews, and pitches with Tiny House Nation accompany us as we visit Elizabeth's alma mater of Notre Dame and I consider confronting the ex-boyfriend who sexually assaulted me in college who now works here. I decide against it, and instead relish time with my queer little family visiting bookstores, Touch Down Jesus, and imagining a college-aged Elizabeth peddling her bicycle through campus.

As we drive toward Ohio, Carl accepts a job offer. He works for a couple weeks, and my mom encourages him to give her his first paycheck so she can dole out his money in increments for groceries to lessen his temptation to binge and get high. He refuses. The day after he cashed his check, Carl drove to work. Next to his office was a Staples. Staples has shelves filled with duster. Carl called and resigned. He chose duster.

Riah transitions to big kid undies at Cuyahoga National Park as the road trip portion of our travels begins drawing to a close. Though Shenandoah was not on our original itinerary, we decide it would be a thoughtful homage to the place that bore us to visit the green hills of the southlands, the place we both were born and raised, albeit in very different ways. As Little Freya trucks toward North Carolina, where I will serve as an Author and Theologian in Residence at a church while teaching fall semester at a university, we pause for one night at that Southern Virginia campground we called home for a month the previous fall. With sippie cups filled with sweet wine, we toast Audre Lorde and embrace an evening of self-care. The adventure is far from over, but it is a fitting way to complete four months of cross-country rambles.

**Compassion.**

As I reflect over those four months, and the entire year we've spent traversing the American landscape searching for the grace of the world, I keep coming back to one of the few icons left in the green plastic bin, Guanyin, Buddhist Goddess of Compassion and Mercy. I painted her quite a few years prior and had published an essay about her before our travels. But I returned to her, yet again, through the lens of so many of the virtues that had been tested, affirmed, challenged, and reinvigorated while roaming. Lorde's womanist ethic of care partners with compassionate care as we recognize Guanyin as an icon for queers, pacifists, and vegans.

Guanyin is the Buddhist Goddess of Mercy and Compassion. In the Lotus Sutras, she originates from a bodhisattva named Avalokitesyara. Avalokitesyara is identified as male in the Lotus Sutras. Overtime, however, Avalokitesyara transitions from being identified as a male to becoming Guanyin, most often portrayed in feminine terms and referred to as "she." Many scholars assert that Guanyin is androgynous and can take on the form of any sentient being. And this is how I've always written about Guanyin, as the divinely androgynous one who is most often portrayed in feminine form.

When I've written about Guanyin in the past, I realize that my placing her into the category of "androgynous" stemmed from my own cisgender privilege. Because I do not view the world through transgender eyes, there are important, meaningful, and revelatory things that I miss; if only I'd read Guanyin's *trans*formative story through her lens of compassionate care, I may have noticed it in the first place.

Upon doing more research on Guanyin and transgender identity I came to realize that she has been and continues to be claimed as a trans icon for many in the transgender community. The overt discrimination and tremendous social stigma against transgender people parallels the way many religious traditions damn, hate, and demoralize their existence in a manner that assaults the souls and violates the lives of countless trans people. In these ways, it is no surprise that many in the trans community find solace in Guanyin: a trans bodhisattva whose true identity is confirmed and celebrated as the Goddess of Mercy. Guanyin becomes a queer icon.

In addition to being a queer icon, Guanyin also functions as an icon for pacifists and vegans. The rich iconography of her image often involves her having eleven heads so that she has more ears to hear all the cries of those who are suffering, or one thousand arms so that she can reach out to even more who are oppressed. Equally profound, Guanyin's iconography involves having webbed fingers, just like the Buddha. Their fingers are webbed so that no one can slip through the cracks of their compassionate love. Guanyin so hears the cries of the universe that no one slips through the cracks into acts of violence. Guanyin's hands are bearers of peace. Guanyin becomes a pacifist icon.

And it is not only humans who remain caught in the webbed fingers of her compassionate embrace, but all beings. In these ways, Guanyin is often portrayed in vegetarian and vegan restaurants as a patron saint of all beings, lover and protector of all animals. Key feminists we can look to for understanding these seemingly disparate connections are Breeze Harper and Carol Adams. In Adams's *Sexual Politics of Meat*, she reminds us of the intricate connections between the subjugation of women and the subjugation of animals. Meat eating is a feminist issue. Adams illustrates this most poignantly in the cycle of objectification-fragmentation-consumption.

In a carnophallogocentric world—one that values white meat-eating men as worthy of the most subjectivity—animals are objectified and denied subjectivity, viewed and referred to as "it." This denial of subjectivity leads to fragmentation, which is most obvious in slaughterhouses, the majority of which are factory farms where animals are slaughtered every twelve seconds and then fragmented by an array of knives at the hands of workers paid unfair wages. In many of these factory farms, animals have no room to even move within their cages, their feet decompose due to standing in their own waste, and the waste that is removed simmers in giant manure lagoons; there are numerous reports of workers drowning in these lagoons. So, the process of fragmentation is demoralizing for animals, workers, and the environment. Fragmentation ultimately leads to consumption where what was once a live animal is now dead flesh on a plate, consumed by meat-eaters.

This same cycle of objectification-fragmentation-consumption applies to women. In media and popular culture, women are objectified and denied subjectivity as objects of lust and desire. We are fragmented in advertising and language as breasts, hips, butts, and thighs are often spoken of as

130

"pieces of meat" or shown without a face or the rest of the body. This fragmentation leads to consumption, not so much on a plate as with the eyes, as objects of male desire. The subjugation of animals and the subjugation of women are inextricably linked in the sexual politics of meat, in a patriarchal society that values the construct of the need for meat-eating more than the reality of subjectivity within the lives of women and animals. With tears pouring from her eleven heads, Guanyin's hands quiver as she holds these realities in her webbed fingers, compassionately carrying the weight of animals and human animals with care. Guanyin becomes a vegan icon.

This is a lot to take in. But it is part of the queering of the American dream. Questioning everything. With one thousand arms, eleven heads, and a heart filled with compassion, something tells me she can handle it. Guanyin: the queer, pacifist, vegan icon of compassionate care. So, I return to this Goddess of Mercy and Compassion anew. The painting and the words remain the same. Her iconography does not change, but her icon status does. It expands, much like her arms, to encompass more, represent more, embrace more. This icon venerated by queers, pacifists, and vegans hears our cries of suffering, and her heart cries out to us:

*Hearing the deep cries of the world,*
*She offered mercies upon mercies*
*Out of her compassionate heart.*

Though they seem disparate to many, my queerness, pacifism, and veganism are inextricably linked. Much like Hawai'i's aloha 'āina movement, the way we treat ourselves, our sexuality, others, animals, and the land cannot be separated, but are mutually informative and reciprocal. It's worth noting, too, that the act of compassionate care and feeling of mercy and love is viewed as *being* Guanyin. Therefore, a merciful, loving, compassionate, caring, and kind individual is understood to *be* Guanyin. In the moments when we show compassion, when we share mercy with all sentient beings, we become the Goddess of Mercy. When we become Guanyin, one less suffering soul slips through the cracks and is instead held in compassionate embrace.

As I toast a glass of wine in the shadows of the Jefferson National Forest after four months of crossing the country from West to East, I ponder how Guanyin would treat Carl. How might she show care to the addict? What is

131

a compassionate response to my lonely brother who refuses to accept the love and help his family offers? Can Guanyin help me see past the addiction that has stolen his heart to witness the little brother who needs love and care so deeply?

These questions weigh on me as we drive to Atlanta to visit my side of the family. I see Carl only once because he doesn't show to celebrate my mom's birthday. And then he fails to show up to celebrate my birthday. And when my mom, Josh, and I all invite him to the Botanical Gardens to see a favorite artist of ours, Chihuly, he never responds. Though I know that addiction takes away a person's sense of self, it is hard not to feel hurt at his chosen absence, and harder to see my mom hurt as only two of her children celebrate her birthday with her, while one was only miles away, drowning in depression and duster. It seems that he will accept none of my offers for help and continues to refuse to open up. We pack our camper and head north. After visiting Elizabeth's mother at a lake in the North Carolina foothills, Little Freya sets up camp for the last time in Boone with Guanyin's compassionate care simmering in my soul. If only my fingers were webbed like hers so that I might scoop up my brother's suffering soul and place him in the healing center of the lotus flower so that he might find peace. I don't want him to fall through compassion's cracks.

Where do you need an ethic of care, beloved? For me, the beauty of the American landscape sustained me as my brother's addiction spiraled out of control. In the face of his addiction, the Pulse massacre, the Brock Turner ruling, and all those daily struggles hurled at queer women, I knew that mere bubble baths couldn't sustain me. Neither could a meditation routine and exercise. Like Lorde, my self-care also needed to examine these systems designed to disenfranchise me and so many others. Dreaming of this dismantling while swathed in a Tolkienesque forest, rereading Lorde overlooking snowcapped mountain vistas, and holding my wife and child's hands, confident in the innate worth of our queer little family while hiking through sand-scorched canyons gave me the care I needed.

We deserve revolutionary care, subversive sister saints. And seeking it out is not selfish. It is necessary. With Audre Lorde holding our tired hands, Guanyin places us in the center of the lotus flower. Rising out of the mud of suffering, we blossom with the lotus, rooted in radical care for self and others. This, I believe, has the power to queer the American dream.

## Chapter 6: Interconnectedness

# Boone and Atlanta:
# Sojourner Truth and Sarasvati

*"Make a burning ground of my heart. That, Thou, Dark One, hunter of the burning ground, may dance Thy eternal dance." -Bengali hymn to Kali*

The same congregation that had hosted an exhibit of my art and offered a couple of my retreats a year prior has invited my queer little family to return, this time plugged in and fully present as an Author and Theologian in Residence. The pastor and I chuckle at this title, given my abandonment of a theos, but it is apt, nevertheless, as I lead weekly book groups based on my recent publication, *Microaggressions in Ministry: Confronting the Hidden Violence of Everyday Church.* The church is also setting into motion our previous conversations about offering a Spirituality for Non-Theists Group. I was invited to lead the inaugural meetings as a motley gaggle of atheists, agnostics, doubters, seekers, Buddhists, pagans, and Wiccan members of the congregation gathered on a scrabble of donated sofas to meditate on the spirituality of our unbelief.

With chocks secured behind Little Freya's tires, we set up camp less than fifty feet from the sanctuary. This solar paneled building is perched on the edge of mountain holler, a quaint sandbox and playground gated along its edge, and a trailer that bore the original church just a gravel lot away. It is a pretty sweet spot to camp. The WiFi is solid. The playground, sandbox, and children's classrooms are flush with toddler toys. The trailer has a shower and bathtub. There are two full kitchens, should our camper feel too crowded. The sanctuary lacks pews, and congregants fold and put away chairs after worship each Sunday, which means our little family has access to instruments and ample dance space six days a week. And, like most churches across the country, it is really only used on Sundays; the community felt strongly that hosting us was an example of being good stewards of their resources. Plus, I can't beat the eight second commute and mountain views.

On our first Monday, we unfurl a roll of painting tape on the sanctuary floor, measuring out the tiny house that will break ground on our Big Island acre in a matter of months. We tape out the small rooms, Riah sitting in his

7x10 rectangle and imagining where his bed, books, toy cars, and stuffed animals would dwell. Elizabeth and I stand in for a DC refrigerator, swinging our arms as pretend doors to make sure there was enough space to walk by. I sit in my taped off 10x10 bedroom on a conference call with producers, contractors, and something called a "story boarder." I keep pinching myself to make sure it was real life.

**Reminiscing and Routine.**

It's no secret that the past fourteen months of travel have been magical. Yoga under a desert moon, whales breaching the surface on long runs along lava cliffs, canoeing as the lone person on Silver Lake, delicious food, breath-taking hikes, immeasurable hospitality...the list of magic could continue. For this, and so much more, we are infinitely grateful. This time of traveling discernment stems from both a tremendous amount of privilege and copious amounts of hard work. Yet, as we hunker again for nearly four months, the butterfly bushes fading into autumnal glory, I begin to acknowledge some of the difficulty that comes with full-time travel with a toddler.

Since many people espouse critiques of social media, blogs, and travelogues by attesting that users portray their lives as utopian and unrealistic, never posting the photos of the Pinterest fails or bad days, I find it important to dispel any kind of belief that this travel year has been counted by days sipping Pina Coladas on the beach while Riah fans us with palm fronds. Unfortunately, we have yet to train him to do this. In sincerity, though these social media critiques are valid and sometimes true, they also overlook the point of taking photos. Who frames a picture of their family sulking on a rainy hike, or everyone landing on a jumping photo rather than in mid-air? I assume that everyone knows—particularly everyone who has ever had a toddler—that every good photo has at least seven bad ones that weren't frame (or post) worthy. Our sharing of our adventure is similar.

There was and continues to be plenty of mundane accompanying the magic. You know all those things that adults typically have to do: laundry, bills, mail, printing annoying paperwork, cleaning the toilet, taxes, wiping up spills? We've still done all those things. Even amidst the magic. The breaching whale doesn't pay my bills for me. The stunning views after a steep hike won't wash my clothes. What makes the mundane, daily tasks of adulthood more challenging is being on the road. This was a choice we made and we don't regret it. We knew parts would be hard. But we didn't envision spending so much money on laundromats that we could have otherwise purchased a washing machine. Now, there would be no place to put said washing machine in our 140 sq/ft camper, and since we typically didn't have power or water, the washing machine would render itself useless. But you get the idea. The simple task of printing and signing a writing contract became comically difficult on numerous occasions when I had to drive 45 minutes into town to find cell service or wifi, then track down a random place that would let me print, and send it back. In our non-traveling lives in a home, or working in an office, this mundane task would have taken about three minutes. On the road, it took three days. Banking, laundry, bathing, cleaning, grocery shopping, shipping, and receiving mail are all things we did regularly in our "normal" non-traveling life, but all these mundane tasks took on higher degrees of difficulty on the road. There were times this tempered the magic. But it was still completely worth it.

Then there was the manual labor and the not-so-glamorous side of full-time travel with a toddler. I'll start by saying that parenting continues to be the most difficult thing I have ever done. Violence, poverty, addiction, divorce, mental illness, a Ph.D., marathons, death, loss, eating disorders, cracked ribs, sexual assault. These are all things that have been challenging parts of my life in various ways, but none have challenged me as much as parenting. I love my kiddo. Riah is curious and silly, adventurous and active, filled with wonder and laughter; I am grateful to be one of his moms. But it's also really hard. Parenting a toddler on the road is particularly difficult. First, you're living in 140 sq/ft and your "home" changes regularly. When it rains nonstop for 2 weeks or mosquitoes eat all your flesh, you have to be particularly creative not to go bonkers. Potty training remains immensely challenging. We have no community traveling alongside of us, so date nights, time alone, or help watching our kiddo is very rare. We are together 24/7. We knew this before we left. And we chose to do this anyway. And we'd do it again in a heartbeat. But that doesn't make it any less difficult.

Because we did this adventure on the super-cheap, we refused to pay to camp most of the time when we weren't doing work exchanges for five months. So, we'd go about two weeks of "dry camping" before paying for a few nights at a fancy campground that had electricity and water. "Dry camping" is the phrase used to describe camping without power or water, often on Bureau of Land Management areas, Walmart or Casino parking lots. Our camper has a battery that keeps it charged for a few days, but none of the outlets are wired to run on the battery, so we couldn't charge any of our cell phones or computers. I cannot tell you the number of hours I spent looking for outlets to charge my phone or battery block; I could tell you, but that would be more embarrassing than telling you about pooping in a bag. And our water holding-tank was usually enough to provide us about 5 days of washing, cooking, and drinking water. Then we had to manually refill with jugs of water in a funnel we cut out of a diet coke bottle. Or we had to get creative. Once I washed my hair in the bathroom of Ben and Jerry's in Burlington, VT. We made deals with the owners of a B&B so that we could use their outdoor shower. We took countless Campsuds baths in the lake. We lugged around heavy water containers and filled them up anytime we found a place with potable water. And we stank a lot, too.

During our times dry camping in not-so-beautiful places like Walmart or Casino parking lots, we still wanted to exercise, so you could find us unrolling our yoga mat in the Walmart parking lot or endlessly running loops around the outside of a casino with Riah in the jogging stroller. There were stunning runs with inspiring views, to be sure, but there were also plenty of times we dodged potholes at a truck stop while sprinting past cat-calling truckers. If a set of queer parents with an active toddler asked if they should take a year to do something similar, we'd tell them "yes." But we'd also say that the beauty and magic is coupled with a lot of challenges that are often minimized by people who think you can do this because your life is perfect or you must be rich. We are neither. But we are pretty damn lucky. If our fortune and wonder may smell slightly of a plastic suitcase filled with piss, that's fine with me.

**Settled.**

Smelling slightly better, overflowing with the amenities of modern life, including a beloved church Washer/Dryer that had eluded us throughout the entire year, we are settled-ish. I'm teaching fall semester at the university where I used to work, which is a ninety-minute drive off the mountain and into the Piedmont. Incredibly fortunate, the department head and dean worked with my wonky schedule so that I can teach all three classes in one day and ensured that I have a little office for prepping, grading, and recovering in between. Rising with stars still speckling an inky sky, I lumber to the church's trailer for a quick shower. As my family continues to slumber, I hop into the car just in time to see the sun rise over the Blue

Ridge Mountains, my ears popping along the Parkway as I wind toward campus. The majestic beauty tempers the length of the drive. Every week, my jaw drops.

I've missed teaching profoundly while traveling, and I relish my early morning sunrises that erupt the mountains in the fiery glow of new beginnings. The campus where I teach is particularly stunning in fall as I tromp through crackling leaves to teach. Women, History, and Myth is anchored in my painting and writing about revolutionary women; Gender, Food, and the Body in Popular Culture articulates the intersectional ecofeminist philosophy my little family endeavors to embody; and Embodying the World Religions is yet another opportunity to grapple with the spiritualities of the major wisdom traditions. These courses, and that revolutionary place bell hooks describes as the most radical space in the academy—the classroom—are more than a good source of income for the fall. They are a gift to a searching spirit who is nourished equally by the grace of the world, the quandary of the classroom, and the creativity in the studio.

The High Country feeds this grace of the world as my queer little family hikes until our hearts are content. The church is providing this strange liminal space to continue questioning my faith. The university offers up the hallowed halls filled with eager (or tired) students. And in that sacred empty sanctuary, I pull my paints and brushes out of storage and begin to paint again. Pele, Hawaiian goddess of the volcano, Hina, Hawaiian goddess of rain and moon, Poli'ahu, Hawaiian goddess of snow on Mauna Kea, Papahanoumoku, Hawaiian mother earth, Oya, orisha of change, Our Lady of Light, Sojourner Truth, Dolores Huerta, and so many others pour from my brush as my body and heart finally have the space to express what I've learned and encountered throughout my travels. The Holy Women Icons Project grows exponentially in that space, our green plastic bin now refilling with new faces, new heart yearnings, the intersections of history, myth, gender, and revolution swirling on my pallet.

**Searching for Sarasvati.**

And I have the opportunity to do what I'd longed to do for so many years. To bring together my love for sustainability, the academy, spirituality, and the arts. After searching across the American landscape for these

137

connections, I discover them where I first began. In searching for Sarasvati, I create her in a tiny camper nestled in North Carolina's High Country.

For years I have been searching for Sarasvati, the Hindu Goddess of Arts, Wisdom, and Learning, claiming her—as much as a non-Hindu can—as my patron saint, the one who guides my path as I navigate three seemingly disparate callings: artist, scholar, and activist. In Sarasvati, these three callings merge. She reminds me that the divisions between fields are our construction; that academics can be creative, art can be holy, and spirituality can engage the mind. These three seemingly disparate callings do not have to be mutually exclusive. Sarasvati certainly wouldn't see them this way.

Sarasvati is the Hindu goddess of knowledge, music, arts, and science. Along with Lakschmi and Parvati, she is part of the trinity of consorts to Brahma, Vishnu, and Shiva. Often depicted on a river or body of water, her name literally means "she who has flow." Hindus pray to Sarasvati for creative inspiration and academic knowledge, but most importantly for divine knowledge essential for reaching *moksha*, or liberation. Her iconography is riddled with symbolic meaning.

Iconographically, her four arms represent the four aspects of human personality: learning, mind, intellect, and alertness. Her white pearls represent the power of meditation and spirituality; her pot of water represents the creative mind and powers of purification; her *veena/vina* (type of guitar) represents the perfection of all arts; and her book is the sacred *Vedas*.

Because her iconography is well-established, years passed before I decided to paint my own icon depicting her image. While she embodies so many aspects of life that are vitally important to my calling, I didn't know if it would be right to paint her in my folk-feminist style. I learned more. The calling persisted. Seated on both the swan and lotus that often accompany her, and surrounded by the deep blues of flowing water, Sarasvati spread her four arms wide, embracing all. Her heart cries out to us:

> *As waters of a river,*
> *So flow knowledge and creativity*
> *From her heart,*
> *Pouring into humanity*
> *Inspiration and wisdom…*

The ways in which Sarasvati embodies the arts, knowledge, and spirituality in her unified and flowing being continues to inspire and challenge me to live fully into these seemingly disparate elements of my own life and calling. Because, once upon a time, before academics created fields and relegated certain questions as only answerable by particular experts, and before we divided science from religion and lost our innate sense of wonder, and before creativity and the arts were dubbed "soft" and "un-academic," Sarasvati reminded us that the arts, knowledge, and spirituality are inextricably linked.

She reminds all of us to make connections otherwise unseen. Her creative heart inspires us to search for and create beauty. Her wisdom emboldens us to ask difficult questions that may not have easy answers. And the ways in which this goddess connects knowledge and the arts with spirituality is very holy, indeed. As I taught college football players what it means to be a feminist, and seminary students how to whirl like the Sufis, as I painted revolutionary women from history and mythology, as I listened and meditated with spiritual non-theists, and as I plucked rainbow chard from the congregational garden, Sarasvati stirred within. This is the life I am creating. A life where the arts, spirituality, knowledge, and a profound respect for the land—the work of aloha ʻāina and indigenous ways of knowing—is lived and embodied on a daily basis. Intersectionality emboldened, from India to a North Carolina mountain holler.

**Accident.**

Each week, I have an opportunity to ponder this intersectionality and my sense of call with the church's pastor, another queer clergywoman envisioning a different world. Weekly, we talk liturgy, vocation, belief and unbelief; together, on hallowed folding chairs we vent and theorize, meditate and plan. During one of our first sessions, when the semester had only begun and my book group at the church was just underway, my dad calls. He doesn't call too often, and given that Carl was living with him, I step out of my meeting to answer.

I was concerned when Carl moved in with our father. Though my dad has fallen in and out of addiction throughout my lifetime, he has an ever-present shoebox filled with prescription pain pills, plenty of liquor, and such an array of guns that our child is not permitted at his home. Though

Carl was without any money to buy duster, he could certainly still raid my dad's stash, steal duster, and become violent with himself or others. He'd already totaled four vehicles at this point. Dad is virtually incomprehensible on the phone.

Carl is in emergency surgery after being rushed to the hospital in an ambulance. I assume this was duster related. Dad insists Carl was clean. Rather, he was carrying dirty dishes down the stairs, clad in the colorful socks he so enjoys. He slipped. A plate split and punctured his eye. In surgery, we'd learn he'd lose his eye forever. A prosthetic could be possible, but it was tremendously expensive, and he was uninsured. A hollow black hole was stitched, and he would soon dub himself a pirate, claiming higher membership in the Church of the Flying Spaghetti Monster. The next morning, I have a full slate of classes to teach, and since it was only the second week, I can't cancel classes. Both parents assure me they'll take turns at Carl's side, as will our youngest brother, Josh. My plan is to teach and then drive five hours to Atlanta to see Carl.

I arise before dawn, the sun turning the autumnal Blue Ridge Parkway gold as I snake toward campus. I teach my morning class with an uneasy feeling in my stomach, checking my phone during break. As I prep for my next class, I begin vomiting. Due to a long history with eating disorders, I can unfortunately handle puking like a champ, so I teach my next class without issue. Sweating in my office, I call my mom to check on Carl. He is on pain meds and will remain in the hospital for many days. When I tell her of my symptoms, she urges me not to come, concerned I could give Carl an infection. I quickly rush to a clinic and am diagnosed with the flu. I foolishly teach my last class (no one else ended up getting my sickness), and drive back to the camper. My mom spoke with Carl's doctors, and they insisted that I couldn't even enter the ward with the flu; it would be too dangerous for Carl and all the other patients.

When Carl is lucid enough to talk, he tells me he plans to accompany my mom on her visit to the mountains to see my queer little family because he feels it would be a beautiful place to recover. I am hopeful. I hurt to see him hurt, to see our family hurt, but we are all hoping this might be some kind of traumatic wake up call. Afterall, when he flatlined from alcohol poisoning ten years before, the hospital bills piled up, he created a plan, got a job, and cleaned up his life. Now this. Upon discharge, though the hospital highly recommended therapy—and offered it in the trauma

140

center—he refuses to go. "Losing an eye is a traumatic event that impacts the rest of your life, and you need help processing it," the doctors and nurses inform him. "I've experienced worse," he responds stoically. The truth is, he has.

**Visits.**

Mom visits us in the mountains. Carl doesn't come. We run in another half marathon, and I live-paint at a Women's Preaching Conference in Durham, again enlivened by revolutionary women doing this work, but lamenting that it is likely a faith tradition I can no longer claim as my own. One amazing woman takes me on an impromptu Pauli Murray mural tour, and shows me the house Murray grew up in. Together, we talk politics and preaching, feminism and faith, non-profits and the revolutionary women who hold all these things together. Intersectionality.

As the election draws closer, Riah's birth parents visit, sleeping on an air mattress in the church's trailer, as we celebrate Riah's third birthday. With Riah finally potty trained, we all hike with no need for diapers in our backpacks. Glory be. After Riah's bedtime, we huddle under blankets outside the camper while livestreaming the final debate. Riah's birth mother can't help but laugh at me. "Angela, I've never seen you so angry. You're normally so peaceful, but watching this is clearly pissing you off." The four of us share similar worldviews and rage against what the presidency could become if Donald Trump is elected. "Surely he won't win," we all agree. There's no way the country would elect a racist, xenophobic, rapist into office. Would we?

Dad visits us in the mountains. Carl doesn't come. He offers us a date night on election day, so Elizabeth and I go to our favorite Italian place and eat under a large television displaying results. We aren't looking too often, confident in Hillary Clinton, devouring our lasagna, toasting our wines, and relishing solo time together. I catch a glimpse of the results. "That can't be right," I insist. "We're on the East Coast, remember," she assures me, "California hasn't rolled in yet." We go to bed uncertain. I check my phone each time I get up to use the bathroom. In the middle of the night, it is confirmed. I sit in bed and cry. Elizabeth wakes up to ask what is wrong and can't believe it when I tell her. "Donald Trump is president. Hillary won only the popular vote."

The shit has officially hit the fan. The next night, our Spirituality for Non-Theists Group met, forlorn. Together, we grieve and console, weep and worry. Many Republican friends are quick to quip, "Why are you worried? Get over it. You lost. We lost last time. We survived. We've all survived the presidents we didn't vote for in the past." Here's the thing, though. We all didn't survive. Black people routinely murdered by the police haven't survived. Indigenous women who go "missing" without trace didn't survive. Queer men dying of AIDS in the 80s and 90s didn't survive. Refugees dying at our borders didn't survive. Women's bodies raped—including by the very man we now call president—well, our bodies may have survived, but our souls can be a different story. Those who claim survivorship do so because of the unexamined privilege of never knowing one for whom life ended due to the oppression, injustice, marginalization levied by politicians. As people of color, immigrants, queers, persons with disabilities, and the folx we call our allies rage and march, fearing the worst, I think of Sojourner Truth. I'd just painted her for a second time and she found sisters nestled in the green plastic bin.

**Truth.**

I've long held that feminism, in order to be true and engaged and practical, must be intersectional. Such is also the case, I believe, for LGBTQ rights. The work of justice for women and LGBTQs must also include justice for other marginalized groups. Because many LGBTQ people are also women, people of color, people with disabilities, Muslims, immigrants, and others marginalized for identities other than their sexuality. Paying attention to these intersections—of sexuality, gender, race, class, ability, religion—and acknowledging that many people have multiple intersecting identities for which they are oppressed is vital to the work of justice. Having painted and sold an icon of Sojourner Truth at my very first exhibit a decade ago, I felt called to paint her anew, with intersectionality guiding my brushstrokes.

Later, in response to Trump's presidency, Trans activist Janet Mock reminded us of the importance of intersectionality in her speech, saying:

*Our approach to freedom need not be identical but it must be intersectional and inclusive. It must extend beyond ourselves. I know with surpassing certainty that my liberation is directly linked to the liberation of the undocumented trans Latina yearning for refuge. The disabled student seeking unequivocal access. The sex worker fighting to make her living safely.*

*Collective liberation and solidarity is difficult work, it is work that will find us struggling together and struggling with one another. Just because we are oppressed does not mean that we do not ourselves fall victim to enacting the same unconscious policing, shaming, and erasing. We must return to one another with greater accountability and commitment to the work today.*

Long before Mock uttered these profound words, and much prior to Kimberlé Crenshaw coining the term "intersectionality" in 1989, another revolutionary lived and dared intersectionally. In the words of Audre Lorde, this revolutionary reminded us that "I am not free while any woman is unfree, even when her shackles are very different from my own." Her name was Sojourner Truth (1797-1883) and she was an African American abolitionist and women's rights activist. Truth was born enslaved, but escaped with her daughter, Sophia. Called to preach a gospel of liberation—in Christ, from slavery, and for women—this intersectional prophet offered a speech at the 1851 Ohio Women's Convention in Akron, Ohio. She is most remembered for this speech, though many believe that the words were re-written by a reporter since Truth, raised in New York, likely didn't use Southern colloquial speech patterns. Nevertheless, it is a speech I assign in almost every class I teach. It is a speech that reminds us of the importance of intersectionality. It is a speech that our country would do well to read. In fact, I would contend that it should be required reading for all Americans.

As myriad wealthy white women rallied to gain the ability to vote, Truth reminded them that she, too, was a woman, saying:

*That man over there says that women need to be helped into carriages, and lifted over ditches, and to have the best place everywhere. Nobody ever helps me into carriages, or over mud-puddles, or gives me any best place! And ain't I a woman? Look at me! Look at my arm! I have ploughed and planted, and gathered into barns, and no man could head me! And ain't I a woman? I could work as much and eat as much as a man - when I could get it - and bear the lash as well! And ain't I a woman? I have borne thirteen children, and seen most all sold off to slavery, and when I cried out with my mother's grief, none but Jesus heard me! And ain't I a woman?*

Over 170 years ago, she showed us what it means to queer the American dream by embracing intersections. Sojourner Truth stands tall, proud, and strong, her heart crying out to us:

*With arms strong*
*Enough to carry*
*The weight of the world…*
*"Ain't I a woman"*
*She cried on behalf*
*Of all those broken and bound.*

Bringing in the spiritual side of things, Truth continued, pointing to a clergyman, "That little man in black over there, he says woman can't have as much rights as man because Christ was a man. Where did your Christ come from? Where did your Christ come from? From God and a woman. Man had nothing to do with him!" Though I feel god slipping out of my grasp, hers is a theology I can affirm. For if God does exist, She is most certainly a trans black woman, dancing wild and free. Truth, Lorde, and Mock are correct, beloveds. It is our duty to work for the liberation of all people, not just the ones whose marginalities are the same as our own.

**Resurrection.**

Reeling from these intersections, I call my little brother on November 23, 2016 to wish him a happy thirty-third birthday. We remain casually upbeat as addiction, eye loss, and duster linger around the edges of our conversation. He tells me of his recovery, how he'll never have an eye because he could never afford a prosthetic, how he would probably be in medical debt for the rest of his life. He thanks me for the colorful socks we mailed him. I ask if he is using and he says no.

"You can't buy duster if you don't have money," he tells me.
"Thirty-three is a big year," I respond.
"Jesus year," he says, coolly.
One's thirty-third is a Jesus year. Because Jesus died at thirty-three. I'm not sure what it is we mean when joke about this. And by "we," I mean we religious folk, or folk mired in the academic study of religion.
"Promise me you won't end your thirty-third year like Jesus did," I implore Carl.
Without missing a beat, he quips, "Resurrection doesn't sound too bad to me."

But we've long abandoned any notion of Jesus' resurrection. If I'm honest, there were only a few brief years—before the full development of my

144

frontal cortex—when I would have adhered to any kind of belief in a bodily resurrection, but even the remaining years of ordained ministry were filled with my sermons about how we—the followers of Jesus—were resurrection incarnate. That love was not killed and buried in a tomb, but lives on in us. And it's possible I might still believe something like that. Because I don't believe Jesus died to appease an angry God to forgive our sins. Rather, he died at the hands of an unjust empire that sought to kill any manifestation of liberation for the oppressed and marginalized. This isn't revolutionary. Most progressive Christian clergy believe this instead of a bodily resurrection. Where I find myself dangling over the edge isn't in listing Jesus as one among many revolutionaries who upset the status quo, but in claiming there is no God from whence he came. An unwed teen mother, perhaps. But a God, I'm not so sure.

I, of course, am not talking about resurrection when I ask Carl not to end his thirty-third year like Jesus. I am speaking of death and crucifixion. A cross of addiction's making, the crossbar mental illness, the nails poverty, and crown of thorns toxic masculinity. Perhaps the spear is personal responsibility, but it takes someone else to pierce with it. Bearing witness is both the gift and burden of clergy, and it was the cross I bore most my life. I bore witness to Carl's hardships throughout childhood, adolescence, and adulthood. Whether it was nearly having his throat slit by robbers at age six, being jumped and beat up in middle school, or flatlining from alcohol poisoning in his early twenties, I was there on the sidelines, bearing witness. As clergy, I bore witness to life and death, births and funerals, weddings and divorces, and all those moments in between that are the stuff of ministry. I haven't seen it all, but I've seen a lot. In hospital rooms with suicidal congregants when the medical staff couldn't fathom I was pastor. In principal's offices when my queer teen congregants had been bullied while the administration turned a blind eye. In chapels when an eight-month pregnant widow hurled herself onto the coffin bearing her husband's dead body. In sanctuaries and leaky baptistries, ducking shoves from angry parishioners, and alphabetically filing hate mail, while comparing death threats with the local imam. I could bear witness to these things, careening through the tomb like the Magdalene in search of some kind of resurrection hope, but I don't think I can bear witnessing Carl's death.

"Promise me," I ask again.
"Resurrection's dope," he concludes.

**Gender.**

With a heavy heart and a call to do and be more, we begin to say goodbye to our beloved little community in the High Country. Leaving behind my Spirituality for Non-Theists Group, a camper now speckled in snow, and a congregation who gave us a goodbye cake with the word "Aloha" scrawled in icing, we drive to Atlanta for one last Christmas at my grandfather's farm before planting roots on the Big Island.

After submitting final grades, we pause briefly at Elizabeth's mother's home on the way to Atlanta. At a playground, we experience the almost constant ritual of Riah making friends with other children. We intentionally chose a gender-neutral name for our child. Riah wears clothing from both the "girls" and "boys" sections of the store, always with his favorite pink or purple sandals, ideal for playing in multiple terrains. While Riah dangles from the monkey bars, a little girl a couple years older runs up to us. We heard her talking with Riah earlier. She kept asking, "Are you a girl or boy?!" Riah would always respond, "I'm a Riah, of course!" Dismantling the gender stereotypes embedded even before birth is incredibly important to us, and one of the myriad ways we queer our parenting.

Gender reveal parties, gendered clothing—which always makes it more challenging to play for little girls—irk both of us. Elizabeth teaches an entire section on this in her Family Ethics course. So, instead of teaching Riah about the gender binary, and training him to believe he was a rough and tumble boy, we have taught him that gender is a construct, and that most of us don't fully know our gender identity—girl, boy, transgender, gender non-binary, gender fluid—until we're a bit older. Whenever possible, we avoid using pronouns unless people specifically request them. Even at age three, Riah grasps this concept that so many parents, preachers, and politicians fail to understand. We are people. We choose our genders. They are not a biological imperative. And the gender stereotypes we heap upon children are harmful to both girls and boys, and especially to trans kids.

The little girl, clad in sparkly heals that prevent her from being able to truly master the climbing structures, puts her hands on her hips and pointed at Riah, "What is *it* anyway?!"
"Oh, that's Riah," I tell her in a cheerful voice.

"But is it a boy or a girl?!" she just has to know.

"That's an interesting question, but it doesn't really matter," I tell her, "what matters is that Riah is fun to play with!"

She stomps away and another gaggle of children invites Riah into a game of tag.

And some parents might hear this story and claim that it's a clear example that children don't have the capacity to understand these complicated concepts. That gender is ingrained and biologically sets us up from the womb to either be leaders or nurturers, strong or sympathetic, aggressive or passive. I call bullshit. The reason this little girl was so intent on knowing Riah's gender was likely because that's the way she's been trained by her parents, teachers, and adults around her. When children don't understand, it's because adults don't do the work to try and understand and communicate such understanding to them. As young as two, Riah got the idea that people are people and the length of their hair, the style of their clothing, the tenor of their voices aren't what's most important. It's whether they are kind, fun, and playful.

As we've played on playgrounds throughout the American landscape, these reactions have been similar. If a child or parent genders Riah as a boy, they often invite him to climb, play tag, or dig in the dirt. If they gender Riah as a girl, they often invite him to play house or store, making artful designs out of sticks and rocks. Riah is happy doing either, but the type of activities children invite him to participate in varies drastically depending on whether they refer to Riah as a "he" or a "she." When assumed to be a girl, perhaps due to the curls in his hair or his pink shoes, parents are more cautious when he plays, often assuming he's incapable of climbing large structures. When assumed to be a boy, perhaps because of his shorter hair and the dinosaur on his shirt, we sometimes have to intervene because parents and children encourage playing war and pretend guns; guns are not toys and a killing someone is not something we pretend to do.

After mama, mommy, and "it," leave North Carolina, we enter into full-on family Christmas mode. This isn't a big modus operandi for our queer little family, but with myriad relatives to squeeze in before moving to the Big Island, visiting is in hyper mode.

147

**Feminist Holidays.**

There's nothing like the holiday season to bring out everyone's least feminist self. In one of the courses I teach—Gender, Food, and the Body in Popular Culture—students are assigned to examine gender roles throughout the holiday season through the lens intersectional ecofeminism. Inevitably, almost every student returns from holiday break with the same assessment: mom, grandma, and a kitchen full of women prepare, cook, and clean every family meal; women do the holiday shopping; men in the family watch sports. Of course, this isn't true of everyone. There are plenty of families who subvert and dismantle stereotypical gender roles, but the holidays seem to heighten these roles, undergirding them with some kind of nostalgic and theological weight that claims that if mama doesn't arduously prepare her famed casserole, the season will be ruined. Otherwise committed feminists find themselves singing carols filled with sexist language and participating in holiday rituals that they would critique any other time of the year. Subversion be damned because we want our traditional family holiday!

I've long struggled with creative ways to subversively approach the holidays as a queer clergywoman, parent, artist, and worship consultant. People like their nostalgic and heart-warming traditions, even when they sometimes smack of patriarchy, racism, and heteronormativity. I've confronted this as a preacher and worship planner, often to raised eyebrows or angry phone calls from congregants who just want to sing the carols without the preacher changing the words, or dismissing the notion of a virgin birth, or hanging enormous paintings of pregnant women all over the sanctuary.

But maintaining our intersectional feminism is important, even in the face of holiday nostalgia. I've always wanted to paint a Holy Woman Icon who could somehow embody a feminist approach to the myriad winter holidays, yet kept elements of that warm nostalgia that is so important in the season. So, this year I painted Our Lady of Light, in an attempt to honor a host of different spiritual traditions that focus on light this winter season.

In the tradition of my ordination, we are not yet celebrating Christmas (despite the capitalist consumer onslaught that has been on full throttle since October). Rather, we are dwelling in the deep blue darkness of Advent, when we wait, long, and prepare for light to be birthed into our world. A candle is lit each Sunday during Advent and the light grows brighter in anticipation of the birth of Christ.

Advent is not the lone holiday that celebrates flickering light growing in the darkness this month. In addition to Advent, Jews will celebrate Hanukkah, a Festival of Lights. Each night a candle is lit as we remember, "such is the way of creation: first comes darkness, then light." This season also hosts the Wiccan holiday of Yule, which marks the New Year and the celebration of the birth of the God as the Winter-born king, symbolized by the rebirth of the life-generating and life-sustaining sun. Yule is a time for ritually shedding the impurities of the past year and for meditating on ways in which you can develop your spirit in the year to come. In addition to Yule, December 21 is also Tohji-taisai, the Shinto Grand Ceremony of the Winter Solstice. Tohji-taisai celebrates the joy of the sun ending its yin period as it declines in strength, and the beginning of the yang period as its power grows stronger and stronger as the days lengthen. The sun is of central importance in Japan, expressing the presence of Amaterasu Omikami, or the Kami of the Sun.

As the days begin to grow longer again, Advent will end, and the Christmas season will begin. Like the brightening of days, the liturgical colors shift from deep blue or purple to bright white or gold. Light is birthed. The sun grows stronger. Emmanuel is with us. As the twelve days of Christmas begin, so too, does Kwanza, a West African holy season where the candles of a seven-branched candelabrum are lit to represent seven holy attributes: unity, self-determination, responsibility, cooperative economics, purpose, creativity, and faith.

Each of these meaningful wisdom traditions holds unique value that should not be overlooked. The last thing I want to do is neglect their uniqueness by combining them all into one holy woman. Whether the lights are coming from the Advent candles, the Menorah, the yang period of the sun, the fire dancers celebrating the Winter-born king, the seven-branched candelabrum, or the Christmas tree, they are providing illumination in the midst of shadows, pointing us toward peace.

I hold out hope for peace. In our country. In my own faithless soul. And with my little brother. Both my brothers meet up with us at my mother's home in Atlanta. Riah gives Uncle Carl a Band-Aid for his eye. Carl wears it with pride as he makes pillow forts with my child. Because of the house laden with weapons, my father and brothers join us at the Treehouse for our holiday celebration. And we drive to my grandfather's farm, that same place where Carl told me he was resigning from his job a little over a year prior. The same place where Carl and I would get into trouble for having childhood muscadine battles as my uncles hollered at us for "wasting fruit that could earn your papa good money." The same place where we uncovered lost treasures in barns littered with mouse droppings, snake skins, and decades of dust. The same place where my grandparents strung up clap-on clap-off Christmas lights in the 80s, as Carl and I shook presents under a tinseled tree. Surrounded by the memories of that log cabin, Carl makes dusty pillow forts with Riah again. I didn't know it would be the last time I would ever see my brother. Hunkered under blankets, they tell jokes in the shadows, memories that remain captured only in the mind of a child who has yet to understand the permanency of death.

Death seems the ultimate intersecting point. It's something every one of us is guaranteed to experience. We all die. Along the way, it is very likely that someone we love will die, too. Between the living and dying, the oppressed intersections within the lives of many make the living so much harder. Racism. Sexism. Ableism. Heteronormativity. Classism. All those isms used to divide and exclude.

Sarasvati teaches us the interconnectedness among fields and disciplines often segregated in our lives, faith traditions, and schools. The arts, spirituality, gender, wisdom, science, knowledge. They are not separate but interconnected. This lesson was vital for me during our time in the High Country. Academic knowledge in teaching, spiritual wisdom in faithlessness, art, and connection with the land fueled those months nestled in a mountain holler. Sarasvati reminds me that I do not have to choose between being an artist, author, academic, or activist; my calling is to all four and I can honor that calling.

And Sojourner Truth's audacious asking—Ain't I a Woman—was intersectionality defined. Not only are the myriad elements of our lives and callings interconnected, as Sarasvati reminds us, but we are connected to the embodied intersections of others, as well. Gender, sexuality, race, class, gender identity, religion, ability, mental health. All of us, in varying degrees, experience privilege in some of these embodied identities, while simultaneously experiencing oppression in others.

With interconnectedness within us and Christmas behind us, my queer little family bids my family of origin aloha as we load our life into an airplane bound for the Big Island. The green plastic bin emptied into luggage as more revolutionary women accompany us across the Pacific, Sarasvati and Sojourner Truth stirring us to make new connections.

## Chapter 7: Resilience

# Hawai'i:
# Frida Kahlo and Goddesses of Grief

*'A'ohe loa i ka hana a ke aloha.*
*Distance is ignored by love.*

Our beloved Unitarian astrophysicist friends have welcomed us back into their little studio while we prep and film with Tiny House Nation. Adjusting to the six-hour time change, the fifty degree weather increase, and the fact that Donald Trump is about to be inaugurated as our forty-fifth president, I eagerly await the creation of our off-grid tiny home, and the beginning phases of our dream of the Tehom Center non-profit eco-retreat center. As I daydream about painting, writing, parenting, living, and creating in this already-becoming space, I think of how we are painting our reality. And I think of Frida Kahlo.

**Creating Your Reality.**

She famously claimed, "I never paint dreams or nightmares. I paint my own reality." Ever the revolutionary, Kahlo insisted that she was born on July 7, 1910, which is three years and one day *later* than her birth certificate indicates. Believing so deeply in the Mexican Revolution, Kahlo wanted her life to begin with the modern life of Mexico. During adolescence, she never showed a tremendous interest in art. But in September of 1925 everything changed. Kahlo was injured while riding a bus that collided with a trolley in Mexico City. An iron handrail pierced her abdomen and uterus. Covered in the gold dust of another passenger on board, she was rushed to the hospital only to discover that she had a broken spinal column, collarbone, ribs, and pelvis, along with eleven fractures in her right leg, a dislocated shoulder, and a crushed and dislocated right foot. It is during the subsequent three months in a full body cast that Kahlo began experimenting with painting in earnest.

It wasn't long before Frida Kahlo and the famous Mexican muralist, Diego Rivera, fell in love. Though she savored her role as the adoring and beautiful wife of the "genius artist," she was also a queer feminist, artist, and political revolutionary in her own right. In fact, one may say that Frida Kahlo was the inaugurator of folk feminist art, emblematic of national and indigenous traditions, offering an unwavering depiction of the female form and experience. One could also claim she birthed the surrealist movement. Upon marrying Rivera, she maintained her own last name, something almost unheard of in 1929. This gesture was indicative of her stance on many issues.

Their marriage was passionate and troubled. Though he was never esteemed as particularly handsome, Rivera was charming and experienced many other lovers during their relationship, including a marriage-ending tryst with Kahlo's younger sister, Cristina. The couple remarried one year after being divorced. Frida, a sexually fluid woman, also pursued other lovers. Most famous among her lovers were artist Isamu Noguchi and dancer/singer/actress Josephine Baker. Like her husband, Kahlo did not feel confined to the boundaries society placed upon married couples, artists, or women in general.

Her reality was riddled with anguish. She suffered physically from her bus accident; she suffered emotionally from her intense love and utter despair enmeshed in her marriage; and she suffered spiritually as a Mexican revolutionary who longed for equal treatment for all her people. This suffering, of course, manifested itself in her painting. In her countless self-portraits, we gaze at one who adorned her body with the classic Mexican dress, which she claimed, "has been created by the people for the people." Ribbons, ruffles, bright colors, jewels, and sashes increased as Kahlo's health decreased, an outward acknowledgment and beautiful defiance of death and suffering. She created this reality with her creative resilience.

As I considered how I might pay homage to this revolutionary queer feminist artist, I knew she must be seated in front of casa azul, the home that birthed her love of painting, the home where she first learned of revolution, the home where she thrived and suffered most. Draped in the dress that connected her more fully with her people and the earth—tierra—Frida gazes back at us, her arms outstretched in a gesture of embrace, as though she is liberating the Mexican people she loved so deeply. Seated in front of the home where she learned to paint her reality, her heart cries out to us:

*Broken and bent*
*Yet her heart soared...*
*Revolutionary, adorned*
*And affirmed,*
*She painted her reality*

Like Frida, my queer little family is painting our reality with resilience and hope. Five hundred square feet of open construction tied only to solar panels, batteries, and rainwater catchment. In this reality, I dream I will paint more revolutionary women, write more books, offer hospitality to marginalized women, and co-parent my child to grow into a peaceful, intersectional, ecofeminist. The eighteen months we've spent on the open road has shaped much of this dream and the form of our tiny home, and though I've loved the untethered hopes of wandering, this tiny footprint of a home is calling me to plant, to paint again, to form roots. Swathed in jungle, serenaded by ocean waves, and filled with resilience, I am creating my casa azul. For one week, I continue to dream. Filming will begin on our eighth day back on the island, and this far-flung dream will become our reality.

**Vomit.**

Sleeping on a floor strewn with two mattresses, a wriggling three-year-old bouncing between them, we awake the night before meeting Tiny House Nation's Story Producer to the sound of Riah vomiting all over the sheets. Though I'd gotten the flu that fall, we are generally a super healthy family. Riah has only been sick once in his life when he caught RSV from my cousin. He and Elizabeth are known for tough tummies. Nevertheless, the sheets and blankets are coated in toddler puke, we don't have access to a washer, and it is 3am. We clean as best we can, comfort our sweet little keiki, and spread crumpled sheets over still damp mattresses, intent on feeling well and fresh when we began our Tiny House Nation debut the next day.

Alas. Riah pukes through the night, though he says he feels "much better and very great" the next morning. With saltines and ginger tucked in our bags, we set off to meet the first of many producers. As Riah splashes through Coconut Island, seemingly resilient to whatever bug wreaked havoc on his insides just the night before, the producer tells us about the filming process and what to expect in the coming week. Just in case, we tell her about Riah getting sick, and she assures us they've had plenty of sick people while filming in the past, and that there will be extra hands to help throughout the week.

We return to our tiny studio excited, anxious, and eager to begin. The next morning, we awake without one ounce of vomit out of Riah. We quickly learn about the bulk of filming for television: waiting. Unfortunately, waiting is the one thing Riah has an incredibly hard time doing. Keeping him clean and occupied between takes is a challenge, especially because we've pared down our clothes to the bare minimum, and a quarter of his now reek of vomit. When the producers inform us we'll need seven different outfits each, we hit the thrift stores.

Fortunately, there are so many kind, thoughtful, generous members of the cast and crew who step in during all the waiting to play, read books, or teach Riah how to use sound and video equipment. Part way through that first day of filming, Elizabeth begins looking a little green. "My stomach really isn't feeling well," she tells me, tucking the battery pack burning her belly toward her hip. "I may have caught Riah's bug." Only moments later she dashes off camera, and 48 hours of hurling begins. She films throughout it all. In our tiny studio, in our partially built house, in a lava tube, at a pottery studio, she pukes and smiles, wipes explosive diarrhea, and chases our wild child. Everyone is accommodating, and I do my best to be a good nurse, though selfishly bummed that none of us is well enough to hang out with John Wiesbarth, Zach Giffin, and the crew outside of filming during this once in a lifetime opportunity.

The producers knew that participating in the Women's March on inauguration day was incredibly important for our family, so they opt to do their own filming that morning so we can attend. Unfortunately, Elizabeth is still blowing chunks. Fortunately, my dad is considering relocating to Hawai'i, so he arrives on island just in time to help with Riah while I march. Clad in my Black Lives Matter t-shirt, a rainbow stole, and sporting a sign that reads, "This Queer Clergywoman Believes Women's Rights are Human Rights: Less Hate, More Aloha" under my umbrella, I march along thousands of others protesting the sexist, racist, rapist now living in the White House. With miniscule portraits of Frida Kahlo dangling from my ears, I march with her resilient spirit, hoping for revolution. Galvanized, I return to our little studio with tummy meds and soup for Elizabeth.

She hasn't thrown up in a few hours and feels the worst of it is gone. Partway through the night, my stomach begins to lurch far worse than Little Freya when she got stuck on that boulder in Oregon. I dash to the bathroom in time to vomit so violently that I hit my head on the toilet. I puke through most of the night and feel marginally better by morning. Throughout the last day of filming, I can be spotted dashing off camera to hunch over, my guts splattering over lava rock. By the time we finish taping, we've all stopped vomiting, and everyone involved in the show agrees that this was the hardest filming they've ever done. This was due in part to torrential rains, and in part to my entire family puking all over the island. The poor sound crew who had to listen to our retching when the mics were on! They also said, hopefully sincerely, that we'd all been real troopers, always ready on time and eager to do what was needed despite the various shades of green on our sickly faces. We decide that when the show aired, the fun game would be to guess which one of us had just run off camera to vomit. Another would be celebrating each time John Weisbarth said the word "ecofeminist," which brought us much professorial pride.

**Squatting.**

As the rains temper and solid food can enter all our stomachs once again, we bid the cast and crew aloha as we enter into this dream phase of our lives, our casa azul, the painted reality we have created. Kind of. Through seemingly minor miscommunications and misunderstandings between working with many different producers, designers, crew, cast, contractor, subcontractors, electricians, solar technicians, painters, and about one hundred other people, a couple details have fallen through the cracks. Namely, our home isn't actually finished. Well, the building is finished, but it doesn't yet have running water or electricity because the solar, water, and plumbing can't be connected until after the home has been approved through the permitting process, which is notoriously long on Big Island. The home was finished enough to film, but it is not necessarily finished enough to fully live in. Legally. We essentially become squatters in our own house.

We figure we've dry camped for over five months already, so we can dry camp in our own house. For a month, we use a bucket for a potty, though a perfectly good eco-friendly toilet and a completely covered septic system sit in their intended places but are not yet permitted and hooked up, laughing at our trembling thighs as we hover uncomfortably over a utility bucket. We fill giant jugs for drinking water and return to a life of searching for showers and WiFi. Fortunately, friends, beach showers, and outdoor buckets provide plenty of opportunities to bathe. For a month, we finish projects on the house, piss in a bucket, and haul our bottles to fill with city water while our rain catchment system overflows, but can't yet be connected to our home. We would go an additional three months without power because solar permitting took longer than anticipated. This also meant we had no refrigerator, so a cooler and camp stove served as our kitchen, though our tiny house was already flush with a beautiful stainless-steel stove and a DC refrigerator that sat useless in those intervening months.

Five thousand miles away, Carl seems to take his traumatic injury in stride, though he continues to refuse therapy or rehab. I talk with him about visiting us soon, too, once he can find another job, get sober, and save some money. He had enjoyed playing with Riah over the Christmas holiday and sincerely wants to visit us so that he could play with his nephew again. Over the phone, we discuss Frida Kahlo as he is also a lover of all things art and all things subversive. I question how she has emboldened such resilience in me, yet he continues to struggle. He is alone in my dad's house without any money or food. My mom takes him grocery shopping, gives him rides to appointments, and includes him in family activities. She continues to encourage him to try rehab. He cooks and texts mom photos of his meals; they shop together where mom diligently walks on the side where he has lost vision to help prevent him from crashing into stacks of produce.

When he texts my mom that he is going to get an $800 tax refund, she asks what he plans to do with the money. He responds, "I don't know." She offers to hold the money for him so she could dole it out in grocery-sized increments, limiting his temptation to binge on duster. He declines. We've known for a year that the end was coming, but there's something about his answer that solidifies it.

Carl stopped responding to calls and texts around the end of February. When he did this in the past, my mom kept constant watch on their family cellphone plan to ensure he was using data. If he was using data, he was alive. This was how she had to measure his life. Late in the evening on March 5, Carl stopped using data.

**The Ending.**

On Monday, March 6, 2017, my mother drove to my father's house after Carl hadn't used data in several hours. She banged on the door, tried to pick the lock, cried out Carl's name, and even threw rocks to try and break a window. She knew that Carl was dead. Mom called the police. An officer came but refused to kick open the door. "Please," my mother pleaded, "I know my son is inside and he's either dying or dead. I have to get to him." The police officer chuckled and responded callously, "The last time I did that it cost me $250 and I don't get paid enough to lose $250." He left and my mom called a locksmith. After my dad called to give permission for the locksmith to remove the lock, my mother opened the door to find my little brother lying dead on the floor in the same spot where he fell and lost his eye. Hundreds of duster cans filled the house. Colorful socks adorned his cold feet.

When the coroner arrived, he said Carl had been dead for nearly 48 hours, which we learned was incorrect as we gathered Carl's receipts and created a timeline for his binge. Plus, he'd used data less than twelve hours prior. He began dusting on February 28 and his last receipt was for March 5, 2017 at 8:58pm. We assumed he overdosed. This was the language we would use at his funeral, in his obituary, and in informing friends and family. But duster can kill you every single time you use it. It's a miracle Carl lived as long as he did, given how much duster he'd used. It simply cut off the oxygen to his brain and he died. That's it. My little brother was dead. No resilience. No creating his own reality. Gone.

After my mother's call, Elizabeth took Riah to a friend's so she could help me pack and process, book a flight and cry. I walked outside. Construction debris and ankle-turning lava rock surrounded our tiny house. With no one home to hear my wails, I grabbed a shovel and began to smash it repeatedly against the lava rock, screaming with a rage unknown to my body and lungs. Even in the moment, when I expected only emotions to remain, my logical brain analyzed my actions, reminding me of every movie scene when the bereaved responded by screaming. I'd always considered it bad acting. I wasn't acting. I screamed for painful memories and lost hopes. The shovel head split from the handle as I dropped to my knees, black rock scraping flesh as tiny drops of blood trickled down my shins. I wailed and wept, coughing out the anger of thirty-three years of fear and worry, choking on the poverty, mental illness, and addiction that plagued so much of my family's life.

My father and I booked flights back to Atlanta as he quickly began his own downward spiral of coping with pain pills, alcohol, and cigarettes. Unable to comprehend my own grief, I contorted my rage-filled body to try and sleep on the redeye flight. I was angry and sad, raging and heartbroken, unable to fathom this new reality my family faced. Staring out the window, I thought of my little brother, and I pondered my own lack of faith. You see, in most stories, this is where God slips through the cracks, the bereaved outraged at an angry God who would take away someone they loved. But that's not what happened here. Faith in a God slipped through the cracks between my fingers a long time ago, replaced temporarily by Goddess, and then by that liminal space where wonder and quandary meet that cannot be named, titled, or believed. I wasn't mad at God for my brother's death. Because I didn't believe a God existed. I was mad at Carl for using. I was mad at society for creating so many systems set on disenfranchising the poor and mentally ill. I was mad at toxic masculinity that never permitted my brother to feel or express his emotions publicly. I was mad at my father for surrounding us with addiction in childhood, leaving us for addiction in adolescence, and failing to take responsibility for it as an adult. I was angry at myself for not doing more, not loving enough, not dropping my life to save my brother. But I'm not a savior, and though I hold some responsibility in the loneliness my brother felt, I knew—even in those early days following his death—nothing I could have done would have prevented this.

As my reddened eyes gazed into the inky blackness through a grubby airplane window, I thought of disenfranchised grief and how, now that I'd slowly given up on the tradition that ordained me, I had no rituals, lamentations, or spaces to hold me in my grief. There are no "ashes to ashes" for non-theists, no promises of resurrection, no karmic reincarnation, no enlightenment. We die. That's it. I needed handles for my grief, so my mind roved the canons of subversive sister saints who fill my work in the Holy Women Icons Project, grasping. I couldn't unpack a green plastic bin filled with their hearts and faces, but I didn't need to, because these women had etched their stories into my heart over many years and many miles. At cruising altitude, they surrounded me, a great cloud of witnesses who know what it means to grieve.

**Goddesses of Grief**

Upon the death of a loved one, most people in the West are offered commodified grief, costly funerals, and stifled feelings pre-packaged as dignified tradition. When deathcare became a commercial enterprise at the turn of the twentieth century, there was what mortician and author Caitlin Doughty calls a seismic shift in who was responsible for the dead. "Caring for the corpse went from visceral, primeval work performed by women to a 'profession,' an 'art,' and even a 'science,' performed by well-paid men. The corpse, with all its physical and emotional messiness, was taken from women. It was made neat and clean, and placed in its casket on a pedestal, always just out of our grasp (Caitlin Doughty, *From Here to Eternity: Traveling the World to Find the Good Death*, 136)."

In all my vocational work, I am constantly asking, "Where are all the women?" when confronted with practical and philosophical dilemmas. And here I was weeping my way across the Pacific, longing for revolutionary women to guide me through the depths of despair. When discerning how Westerners grieve, I cannot help but notice the correlation between the industrialization of deathcare and the erasure of women's leadership roles in the grieving process. Stepping back to take a long view, one discovers myriad empowering women, goddesses, and saints associated with grief across wisdom and cultural traditions. Uncovering the histories, legends, and myths linked to these grief goddesses just may be what the West needs to heal, to feel, and to grieve again. It may even be part of queering the American dream. Myriad women, goddesses, saints, and subversive sisters filled my mind and heart.

In Mexico, La Llorona—the weeping woman often associated with horror stories following the drowning of her children—has been reclaimed by some Chicana feminists to wail so that our voices may be heard. Santa Muerte, or Holy Death, is a folk goddess who heals, protects, and delivers the dead to the afterlife; according to author and mortician, Caitlin Daughty, Santa Muerte's subversive power is associated with outlaws, the poor, and LGBTQ folks. Mictecacihuah is the Aztec Queen of the Underworld who watches over the bones of the dead and presides over funeral rites. These women remind us to feel our emotions fully as we grieve.

160

In Haitian traditions, Oyá is the Orisha of violent storms, death, and rebirth, residing in cemeteries and aiding in all transitions, whether living or dying. Mama Brigitte is a death loa who protects gravestones marked with a cross. These women remind us that death is one of life's many transitions.

Hailing from the United States, Saint Elizabeth Anne is the Catholic patron saint of grief. Weetamoo was a Pocasset Wampanoag Chief whose legacy is present throughout the National Day of Mourning, an annual protest organized by the Native Americans of New England. Weetamoo, in particular, reminds us of the power of corporate grief.

Frigga, the Norse goddess who dedicated her life to protecting her son, Baldur, weeps tears that become mistletoe berries after these same berries kill her beloved child. Borghild, a Norse goddess who, in seeking to avenge her brother's death, poisons and kills his murderer. These women remind us that the loved ones you have lost always remain with you.

Nephthys and Isis are the Egyptian goddesses of funeral rites, their wings and wails resembling a falcon as they carry departed souls into the afterlife. These women remind us that it's alright to weep.

The tangled Greek myth of Demeter, Persephone, and Hecate evoke grief, as Demeter is so overcome by her daughter, Persephone's, descent into the Underworld, that she dares to rescue her, aided by Hecate. These women remind us that deep love is a vital part of grief.

In Turkey, Rumi's daughter-in-law, Fatima, becomes the first woman to lead the Mevlevi Order of Whirling Dervishes; donning her death shroud as a whirling cloak and placing a hat symbolic of a tombstone on her head, she whirls, each turn evoking bodily surrender to the Beloved. Fatima reminds us that death is always with us.

In Japan, the Buddhist Goddess of Compassion, Kannon, has webbed fingers so that no sentient being can slip through the cracks in her hands as she places each departed soul—and perhaps those grieving their deaths— into the center of the lotus flower. In Japanese mythology, Izanami-no-Mikoto is a goddess of creation and death, her name literally translating as "she who invites" life and death. These women remind us that we are held in our grief.

161

The Hindu goddess Kali is known as a destroyer, dancing atop her consort, Shiva, the creator and destroyer of life. With severed heads forming a ghastly garland around her neck, she does not kill for violence, but to destroy the ego. Kali reminds us that destruction is an imperative part of life.

The Igbo goddess Ala rules the underworld as goddess of morality, fertility, and creativity, holding deceased ancestors in her womb; her name translates literally as "ground" because she has powers over the earth—above and below—and is the ground itself. Ala reminds us that our ancestors are a part of who we are.

Hine-nui-te-pō is the Maori goddess of the night and death, and ruler of the underworld; her love and passion create the red colors in each sunset. Hine-nui-te-pō reminds us that passion can create beauty amidst grief.

Finally, Our Lady of Sorrows is Jesus' mother in the Roman Catholic tradition. With seven swords piercing her heart, representing the seven sorrows associated with her child's death, she weeps in processional each year during Holy Week. These women remind us that we do not grieve alone.

These are merely glimpses into the rich lives, legends, and legacies of these grief goddesses who offer us strategies for coping with grief. No matter where this grief and rage would take me, I was confident that I was not alone, but that a bold canon of grieving women were before, beside, and behind me. With these subversive sister saints upholding me, my body resting in the most twisted of yogic asanas somewhere between Hawai'i and Atlanta, I fell asleep.

**Vigil.**

I arrived in Atlanta in time to weep with my mother and Josh. We met my dad and his cousin at the funeral home. Dad was clearly not sober. Could I blame him when his son lay frozen and organless one room over? We discussed the exorbitantly expensive fees associated with even the most meager packages, agreeing on cremation. Mom gave the funeral director a pair of Carl's jeans and a new shirt with matching colorful socks she'd purchased on his behalf. "Aren't those just going to be burned up?" dad asked, always keen to save a dollar. "Carl was so modest," she said, resolute, "he wouldn't want to say goodbye undressed."

Dad, his cousin, and Josh left to clean duster cans out of my dad's house. Dried vomit streaked across the dash of my dad's dented car from where Carl had driven, and apparently crashed, days before his death. Dad couldn't handle seeing Carl before he was incinerated. "Seeing him covered in blood with a gaping hole where his eye should be was already too much for me," he said. I understood. It was all too much. Mom and I walked to her car as I noticed crowds of my former congregants leaving a funeral. I couldn't see them now, over a decade later. Not like this. I asked my mom one last time whether she wanted to see Carl's body. She changed her mind. We both did. We went back into the funeral home.

After several moments of preparation, assuming he was dressing Carl's body in the clothes my mother had given him, the director invited us to go into an icy room one at a time. When I walked in and saw my little brother's lifeless body, with his arms neatly crossed on a cold metal table, I flashed back through thirty-three years of memories. I sang and hugged him like he never allowed me in life, feeling the weight of his bones, and kissing his stitched eye.

As we left the funeral home, mom needed to stop by a store to exchange a pair of shoes for the funeral, which was only a couple days away. Next to the shoe shop was an office supply store, the kind Carl frequented often during binges. I walked inside and found the section of duster. Rows upon rows of shelves neatly stocked with the drug that killed my brother. It's not truly a drug, mind you. The cans hold multiple warnings about the dangers of sniffing, huffing, or using the duster for anything other than spraying dust. I stood vigil there, the glossy cans with their tiny affixed red straws glaring back at me in contempt. "Fuck you," I muttered quietly. Part of me wanted to scream, to overturn the shelves, to smash the car into the store, crumpling the cans into the dust they'd created as my brother's body burned to ash only miles away. I didn't, of course. Instead, I kept silent vigil as a woman requested help selecting printing paper from a store associate and a man smacked gum far too loud while testing office chairs.

Fuck.
You.

I called Josh. He was sitting in Carl's desk chair staring at his disgustingly dusty computer. "The irony," he sighed. I told him I was grasping a can of duster in my hand, holding vigil at an office supply store while mom shopped for shoes. He said he was holding a can of duster in Carl's old room while dad and his cousin filled trash bags full of cans downstairs, drinking bourbon with abandon.

"Part of me wants to try it," he said solemnly, "you know, to see how he felt."

"Don't," I told him.

"I won't," he said.

"Me, too," I told him.

"Don't," he responded.

"I won't," I promised.

"I love you, little brother."

"I love you, big sister."

**Funeral Rites.**

Hacking into Carl's computer and phone took Josh a little over twenty-four hours, which was actually quite impressive considering how cyber secure Carl was. We contacted his friends and coworkers, finished planning the funeral, which was a small family affair at my grandfather's farm. My mom and I drove to the farm with Josh in the backseat, his incinerated older brother nestled on his lap. The March day began warmer than expected, but the clouds rolled in and temperatures dropped as we arrived at the log cabin. My aunt had cleaned and taken care of everything. Ferns and flowers surrounded a small table covered with photos of Carl, the muscadine vineyard sprawling scraggly in the late winter background. She found a podium for me to use, and folding chairs were arranged into neat rows across the front yard.

After nearly punching an uncle who, with concern for my mom's health, said that maybe this was a blessing, it was nearly time to begin. Dad and his cousin had not yet arrived. A few moments later, dad stumbled out of his cousin's car, slurring something about Xanax and holding a one-of-a-kind bottle of Jack Daniels. It was from the Rodriguez side of the family with a note affixed, "For retirement." I looked at dad's cousin, knowing he would hold my dad together throughout his spiral, and that he offered up his savored unopened and not-yet-realized retirement gift so my father could toast his dead son. "Please keep him safe," I asked him, "none of us can handle another Carl dying." Dad's cousin nodded, always present the moment anyone in the family needed anything, but most especially my dad. They weren't just cousins, but brothers, raised in the system together as Mexican outlaws in the lands of North Carolina poverty. Cuz knew. He knew how to give dad the space he needed to grieve in his own way, while simultaneously keeping him alive.

Cuz couldn't prevent him from acting a fool at his own son's funeral, though. While my words sound heavy with judgment and resentment, I say them also acknowledging that I cannot fathom the loss of my child, and it's not my place to contend propriety over my father's methods. He stumbled over chairs, his buttons askew, much like his late son during the nadir of his addiction. When family shared memories, dad told stories that would have caused social services to take away his parental rights, yet he found appropriate to memorialize his son. Accidentally lighting Carl on fire while using fix-a-flat on a motorcycle tire while smoking or sending him over a cliff on an illegal three-wheeler were stories of a fun-filled childhood in my father's eyes. His childhood was stolen from him by poverty and a negligent mother, so I can't blame him for not knowing how to parent, but that day I was angry that he failed to see how Carl simply followed in his addicted footsteps. This time, dad was unable to put out the fire. Carl was nothing but ash.

With a colander on my head, I welcome the gathered to my little brother's memorial:

*We are gathered in memory of Robert Carl Yarber who died of an overdose on March 6, 2017 at the age of 33. As most of you know, Carl was not average or traditional, so this service will not be average or traditional. We sit in the beauty of his grandfather's vineyard, a mainstay and source of joy throughout Carl's life. From the earliest of childhood, we shared many fun times on this farm, including the day when Carl and I herded all 27 of granny's wild cats into papa's work truck. Or the time Carl, at age six, convinced papa that he could solve a Rubik's cube in under 5 minutes. While I provided a song-and-dance distraction, Carl snuck out to peel all the stickers off the cube and match each side. Needless to say, papa thought Carl was a genius. Throughout childhood, adolescence, and adulthood, this was a place of comfort and family for Carl because he loved and cared for his family very much, even if he had a difficult time showing it.*

*Non-traditional gathering place: check.*

*Not only was Carl non-traditional, he was also non-religious, so we will respect that with this service. As a professor of religion, Carl could hold his own with me when discussing the nuances of world religions and of Christianity, and I would dare say he knew more about Christian history, scripture, and theology than most people who profess the faith. But organized religion and piety were not for Carl, so he opted instead to study them and parody them with the Church of the Flying Spaghetti Monster. Started as a protest to right-wing discrimination, the Church of the Flying Spaghetti Monster holds a light-hearted view of religion and jokingly calls its adherents "pastafarians." As such, the colander is a highly esteemed satirical symbol…you know…because you use it drain pasta. So, we have one here and I plan to wear it to keep me from wailing. And you can, too, if you wish to share a memory of Carl. If this seems blasphemous or heretical to you, you don't have to do it. As an ordained clergywoman, I think it's pretty damn funny.*

*Non-religious satire: check.*

*So, with open hearts and minds, gathered among the family who Carl loved, bring whatever you are feeling into this place—grief, sadness, anger, relief, rage—and let us remember Carl.*

*I invite you to close your eyes, take a deep, full breath, and center yourself in this moment.*

*Aware of the time each of our words occupy in the space, we have two different times for anyone to share about Carl. At this time, we're invited to share memories, particularly fun, joyful, or funny, of Carl with one another. The colander will serve as our "microphone" of sorts. You may opt to wear it on your head if you're so inclined, or to simply hold it in your hand. But whoever has the colander speaks, and everyone else listens. And if Carl's immediate family thinks you're talking for too long, or making the memories about you rather than Carl, we will take the colander away from you, which Carl would find absolutely hilarious. We'll reserve the last memories shared for his immediate family if we so choose. After these fun memories and the eulogy, we'll have a time for anyone to share words of comfort, but for now, let us share those memories of Carl that bring us most joy…*

*Eulogy*

*Carl hated having his picture taken. Since childhood, he skirted the camera, or if you were lucky, smiled unwillingly or flicked you off in the photo. Perhaps it is the existential angst caused by an early death, but I cannot help but think there is something deeper at work than Carl merely not wanting to pose for a picture. I think there was nothing about Carl that could be captured or contained. With a penchant for uniqueness and a deep*

166

*disdain for labels, a photo could not capture Carl's essence, nor could descriptors. He was not one to share feelings, emotions, or even very many thoughts—though his opinion was pretty easy to find, even if you didn't ask for it. He sometimes joked that taking a photo would steal his soul.*

*A tough one to crack, Carl typically had a rough exterior. One could even call him a supreme asshole at times. And such a descriptor is certainly fair. Addiction, mental illness, and a life punctuated by violence can do that to a person. And though Carl's life was filled with profound love and beauty, he also had a pretty rough go.*

*Some who follow the Stiener philosophy contend that the way you were born impacts the rest of your life. While I'm not sure if this is any kind of universal truth, it certainly held true in Carl's life. With the umbilical cord wrapped around his blue face, Carl burst into the world 33 years ago close to dead, nearly killing our mom in the process. Throughout his life, Carl continued to experience hardship. At age six, when our apartment was broken into, it was Carl who found himself at the other side of a robber's knife. Upon biking home from first grade, it was Carl who was jumped and beaten up. And again while trick-or-treating as a middle schooler. And bullied for being fat in high school. These assaults changed Carl. The sparkle in his eyes never faded, even after losing one of his eyes last year, but his fragile soul was forever altered by the pain he endured.*

*Coping is a difficult thing to do, so Carl turned to drugs or alcohol. He loved and he cared and even dreamed, but he was so tormented that life was often too difficult to bear. Depression can do that to a person. It doesn't make them weak. Or bad. Or wrong. It makes them human and fragile and beautiful. And so deeply missed. Inside Carl's being, he held the capacity of all humans: to behold deep beauty and profound love, and to hate and hurt others; holding both these realities simultaneously was torment for him.*

*I don't know if you were aware of this, but Carl didn't have functioning tear ducts. He couldn't produce tears. When he "cried" as a child, which was most often the fault of his older sister, he simply contorted his face, plunged his lower lip outward, and wailed as his face reddened. You would swear there were tears pouring out of his grimaced eyes, but there weren't. Because Carl literally could not cry. I am convinced that Carl felt so truly, so deeply, so profoundly, that dealing with his feelings and emotions—unable to erupt outwardly—was simply too much.*

*Lest we let anger simmer too long, let us also remember the glimpses of kindness and generosity that poured from Carl's uncrying eyes. So often behind the scenes, Carl was the first to show up to help when one of dad's cars broke down for the 87th time. He was there to protect his big sister when her church went sour and deacons broke into the*

167

*parsonage where I lived. He was there for surgeries and sicknesses in the family. And he would often surprise you, when without flourish, he presented you with the most thoughtful gift for your birthday or Christmas. Vegan, fair-trade, organic truffles…surprise, Ang. The comic book or graphic novel missing from your collection and almost impossible to find, here you go, Josh. Reservations at a fancy restaurant at a table with the best view, with Carl seated so that everyone else could see and he couldn't, happy birthday, mom; I'll pick up the tab. Another fire, breakdown, rehab, I'm there, dad. And, little nephew, let me play, and laugh, and build with you, showering you with the most inappropriate and noisy gifts sure to annoy your moms. Uncle Carl loved Riah. And he loved all of you. In fact, one of his friends and colleagues said that, though Carl rarely shared anything personal, the personal things he did share was his love for his mom, dad, sister, brother, nephew, and grandfather, sometimes bragging about his beloved family while sharing muscadines with coworkers.*

*His death is painful and difficult to grieve, to be sure, but also tremendously complicated. For Josh, he was the older brother you always wanted, but never really had. For me, I'll always want to know what Carl was thinking or feeling, and I never get to find out. For dad, he bore your name and your addiction, and was so much like you it's frightening. For mom, you spent 33 years—most of it as a single mom—filling his life with beauty and goodness; as a mom, I cannot imagine the pain of losing my child. I know that both mom and dad would have done anything to take away Carl's torment, and you did everything in your power to try and save him. But addiction is a savage, relentless beast that rips families apart without remorse, and is nearly impossible to overcome.*

*But Carl wasn't just an addict and, though addiction has stolen his life, I refuse to let it steal his memory and define the life he lived. In the words of my mother, Carl was "brilliant, handsome, sarcastic, witty but carrying a great pain that he never shared with anyone." Regarding Carl's brilliance, after one of Carl's former bosses compiled a list of over twenty friends and colleagues who adored him, he told me:*

*"Carl's story always entertained me. He started in Customer Service. Those who knew Carl, recognize how silly that sounds. The company noticed he had a knack for details, so they took him off the phones, gave him a book about Comparison Shopping Engines, and off he went. Inside a few months, he had mastered it so well, he was driving more revenue than the entire Call Center. Carl had talent, but never believed that himself. He was smart, but didn't think of himself that way. His style wasn't always textbook, but Carl was crafty. He could find his own way through the maze — even though his path was uncommon."*

*As I linger over Carl's uncommon path, I will savor our late nights planning Daylight Summer Minicamp as adolescents. I will remember the man who, when many other families shun and exclude and hate, loved his sister as she came out as gay by saying, "You're dating Elizabeth. Damn, I was planning on asking her out." He's the brother who conspires with Josh to flick you off while you're officiating your grandmother's funeral because he knows that's the only thing that will keep you from crying.*

*Scientists tell us that we are descendants of stars. That we are quite literally made of stardust. I saw that twinkle in Carl's eye. And, while it may not be the most philosophically or theologically or scientifically sound, I'd like to think we return to the stars, too, that Carl's spark hasn't died out, but has found a new location in a place where nothing and no one can capture him, where he can seek and love unencumbered by the skin that bound him. For when I look in wonder at the starry night, I see the same twinkle that filled his eyes.*

*From stardust you came, beloved brother, and to stardust you return.*

Resting in one of my late grandmother's handkerchiefs, I scattered my brother's ashes at the base of the vineyard, the wind rushing fragments of his eviscerated bones among the muscadines, the trees, the family, the naked blueberries bushes, the skies, the clouds, and eventually, the stars.

*Since we have shared fun memories of Carl, now is a time for anyone who wishes to share words of comfort, bearing in mind the inner circle of his immediately family who is grieving most deeply. As such, we reserve the last words of comfort for his immediate family. We'll use his beloved colander again, so that whoever holds or wears it may share from their heart...*

*Josh and I are going to read a poem penned by Catullus as he traveled to bring funeral gifts to his dead brother. After we finish reading, we will close with a toast, so Cuz—who Carl respected so much—will pass out drinks. From a one-of-kind bottle Jack Daniels, we will toast Carl from shot glasses Josh has collected for nearly twenty years. If you are not so inclined to drink the shot, you can still toast. I don't imagine we'll have a problem finding someone to drink it on your behalf.*

Holding Josh's hand under the trembling March clouds, we alternated lines, memorializing our dead brother with the poem Elizabeth recited from memory in Latin during one of my weeping sessions before I left the Big Island.

169

Funeral Rites by Catullus

*Carried through many nations and many seas,*
*I arrive, Brother, at these miserable funeral rites,*
*So that I might bestow you with the final gift of death*
*And might speak in vain to the silent ash.*
*Since Fortune has stolen you yourself from me,*
*Alas, wretched brother stolen undeservedly from me,*
*Meanwhile, however, receive these which in the ancient custom of our parents*
*were handed down as a sad gift for funeral rites,*
*dripping much with fraternal weeping,*
*And forever, Brother, hail and farewell.*

The family raised our glasses and toasted my little brother. My cousin's husband, now several years sober, handed me his full glass with a look of innate understanding in his eyes. As we embraced, I thanked him for having the courage to attend. "It could have just as well been me, Ang," he told me in his drawlingly handsome accent, wet eyes softening his tough exterior. With a curt nod, he took my cousin's hand and walked into the log cabin for refreshments.

The next few days were a blur of packing and sorting as I loaded up to return to my own queer little family in Hawai'i, our adventure of full-time travel now officially over and this new season of grief suffocating my breaking heart.

**Goodbye.**

I've been sitting for twelve hours-worth of flying between Atlanta and Hilo, but any chance of relishing the delights of flying without a toddler in tow— reading books or magazines at leisure, writing, watching a movie without interruption, not sharing my snacks—have been plagued with grief. Usually airplanes and airports are my best offices where I accomplish the most efficient writing, deadlines met far in advance at cruising altitude. The strangely confined space and time nourishes my creativity. But this flight is different, and I imagined it would be. I cut and paste notes and slides for upcoming work in Oahu. I tediously type out labels for my art show.

I suppose I'm productive, but not the least bit creative, as though grief and loss and profound sadness and rage have sucked out every ounce of creativity inside me. Between monotonous projects on the computer, I gaze out the window as snow-capped mountains transition into endless sea. I think about how much Carl hated flying and made fun of my love for travel. I think of how much of the world there is left for me to explore, and how Carl won't experience any of it. I wonder if he even wanted to, or if his apathy was merely a shield for the emotions and desires he never shared.

Chasing the sun, we fly directly into the sunset, the glowing magentas and fuchsias lingering longer as we move westward. With tears rolling over my cheeks and streaking the grimy window, the sun finally sets as we begin our descent into Hilo. With a sliver of deep crimson along the otherwise inky horizon, I glance up into the night sky through the tearstained window, and a single star guides our landing. From stardust you came, beloved brother, and to stardust you return. And forever, Brother, hail and farewell.

The adventure continues...

**Conclusion**

# Reflections on Resilience and Radical Imagination

How have you shown resilience in your life, beloved? Though our stories are unique and sufferings particular to our own lives, we have all experienced grief, loss, and trauma, and we all must find ways of coping in order to radically imagine a better world. Personally and collectively. Frida Kahlo's resilience shined forth as she dared to paint in a full body cast, as she continued to create after bleeding fetuses from her broken body, as she loved outside the binaries the world gave to her, as she dressed and dreamed in solidarity with her beloved Mexico. And her resilience in the face of all this suffering—the way she created beauty amid despair— emboldened my own resilience in the face of hardship.

Kahlo's resilience provided painted portals to access the grief goddesses who carried me through one of the most gut-wrenching experiences of my life: my little brother's death. I believe that, even if I still claimed the religious tradition of my ordination, I would still need these global grief goddesses to fully mourn. The ability to grieve—embraced and emboldened by these grief goddesses who suffered alongside me—gave me the resilience to continue living, dreaming, and radically imagining a better world.

I write now, four and half years after my brother's death, and though life has been challenging at times, I can thrive because of the revolutionary women who paved the way before me. As my grief has morphed and changed over the years, other struggles and beauty entered my life. My mother's cancer returned. My family continued living below the poverty line. We opened our tiny off-grid home to a foster child with a traumatic brain injury and adopted her into our queer family. My struggle with mental illness deepened as I entered a facility for full-time eating disorder treatment. A pandemic hit. Life turned upside down. After five years calling Hawai'i Island home, my queer family moved to be closer to medical facilities that can better serve our daughter and to extended family who can support us. Yet I continue to evoke radical imagination as I queer the American dream. But I don't do so alone.

172

Rather, the lives, legends, and legacies of these revolutionary women dream with me, emboldening me to radically imagine a more just and beautiful world. From a global pandemic to the Women's Wave, Black Lives Matter to the popularity of Queer Eye, we are finally beginning to see the world waking up to injustice and questioning the systems comprising a pre-Covid-19 "normal." We are in nothing short of a revolution, and historically underrepresented women are becoming emboldened to use our radical imaginations to subvert an American dream that wasn't working for everyone.

During my years teaching worship and liturgy to seminary students, we called this eschatological imagination. Ritual, worship, and liturgy rooted in the here and now, rooted in social justice, and imagining a more just and verdant world. The eschaton, or end, is too often the focus in religious traditions. How to avoid hell. How to enter heaven. And for too long, straight, white, male Christians have pushed everyone else to the margins, ensuring that they'll "understand it better by and by," that "when the roll is called up yonder," the meek will inherit the earth, those long suffering servants rewarded in a *king*dom called heaven. Eschatological imagination says that's not enough. It's not enough to suffer on earth and be rewarded after death. Eschatological imagination demands that believers bring heaven down to earth. The primary example of this eschatological imagination is the brush harbor scene in Toni Morrison's *Beloved*. Baby Suggs, holy, leads the enslaved to a clearing for worship—laughter, dance, song, and tears finding common ground on brown earth—as she tells them, "the only grace you can have is the grace you can imagine." If you do not dare to imagine it, you will never have it. Not just some day. Here and now.

With the grace of God and the theological notion of eschaton a memory, radical imagination dances its way into the cleared-out space of my faithless heart. There, with the revolutionary women who have guided me, we dance, and in Morrison's words, "long notes held until the four-part harmony is perfect enough for our deeply loved flesh." We are so deeply loved, and we deserve to be treated as such. Because we have within us the radical imagination to dream a better dream. And, together, we have the capacity to make this dream a reality.

When the political climate causes us to fear, remember Lilith and Jarena Lee, and take courage. In those moments when we doubt our callings, or

173

worry that we cannot affect the change we dream of, remember the integrity of Sophia and Freya Stark. As a global pandemic reveals the depths of white supremacist cisheteropatriarchy, remember Mary and Pauli Murray, and dare to hope. In those moments on the borders of inclusion, remember Guadalupe and Gloria Anzalduá, emboldening creativity. As the injustices perpetuated against the least among us cause us to rage, embrace Pele and Dorothy Day, reminding women, in particular, that rage is a vital part of transformation—of self and the status quo. When we are so drained that we feel we cannot care for self or others, remember Guanyin and Audre Lorde, and embrace an ethic of care. As the world pulls us apart, ensiling our identities to create an us-against-them mentality, we remember Sarasvati and Sojourner Truth, embracing our interconnectedness. And when grief and trauma sucker punches us and we find ourselves gasping for breath, we remember Frida Kahlo and the goddesses of grief who ensure resilience enough for all.

Courage. Integrity. Hope. Creativity. Rage. Care. Interconnectedness. Resilience. These virtues—and the women and wandering that made them possible—usher in a revolution of radical imagination. What is the new American dream you are imagining, subversive sister saint? For yourself? And for all people?

Can you imagine living in a country where black lives truly matter? Where children are not forced into border cages because their parents dared to dream of a better life? Where people believe women? Where queer families are treated equally? Where the earth is honored and respected? Where anyone can earn a living wage and have access to healthcare? Where everyone is inspired by their surroundings? Where the American dream is queer enough for all?

Can you radically imagine a better life for yourself? Where exhaustion doesn't dictate your decisions? Where the status quo doesn't harness your dreams? Where you don't have to be part of a perpetual rat race in order to survive? Where anxiety doesn't hamper your joy?

It doesn't have to be this way, subversive sister saints. Eighteen months of meandering the country from Vermont to Hawai'i—and virtually everywhere in between—with sixteen revolutionary women beckoning me onward has taught me that I cannot accept a prepackaged dream that marginalizes and excludes so many. And neither should you. There are revolutionary women behind you and radical imagination within you emboldening you to queer the American dream. Will you accept this emboldening?

## A Word from the Author

Thank you for reading this book and daring to queer the American dream. It is a tremendous help to authors for readers to leave an honest review on Amazon.com
Given that all book sales go to charity, and reviews lead to more sales, and more sales means more donation, your review is like a little donation to turn books to bread for Parson's Porch Publishing and to fund the Tehom Center non-profit.
Want to learn more, take a course, or go on a retreat inspired by *Queering the American Dream*, or purchase artwork based on the book (with all sales benefiting the Tehom Center non-profit)? Go to www.tehomcenter.org

## Acknowledgments

## About the Author

Rev. Dr. Angela Yarber is the award-winning author of eight books and a highly sought out artist and public speaker. With a Ph.D. in Art and Religion and over a decade as a professor of women's, gender, and sexuality studies, she is the Executive Director of the Tehom Center, a non-profit teaching about revolutionary women through art, writing, courses, and retreats. Her art and writing has been featured in Ms. Magazine, NPR's Progressive Spirit, the television show Tiny House Nation, and at Maya Angelou's memorial celebration. All author royalties from her book and art sales go to her non-profit, Tehom Center. Visit www.tehomcenter.org